AMS
TER
DAM

Travel with Marco Polo Insider Tips

INSIDER TIP
Your shortcut to a great experience

MARCO POLO
TOP HIGHLIGHTS

BEGIJNHOF ⭐1
Need a break? Amsterdam's oldest *hofje* is a little oasis among the hustle and bustle.
📷 *Tip: At 9am on a Monday morning, you will have the courtyard to yourself.*

➤ p. 37, Sightseeing

NIEUWMARKT ⭐2
Glorious in its diversity. Around the old weigh house, you can eat nasi goreng, *bierties* and lots of Gouda.

➤ p. 33, Sightseeing

GRACHTENRING (CANAL RING) ⭐
There is no better place to take a stroll in Amsterdam than along its grand central canals, which are named after emperors and princes (photo).
📷 *Tip: From a canal boat at the point where the Regliersgracht meets the Herensgracht, you get a view of seven bridges at once.*

➤ p. 39, Sightseeing

WESTERTOREN ⭐
Climb the tower for a view over the rooftops, while Rembrandt rests in the church below.
📷 *Tip: To get a panoramic shot of the Jordaan, to the west of the church, make sure you climb the tower in the morning.*

➤ p. 40, Sightseeing

RIJKSMUSEUM ⭐
From Rembrandt's *The Night Watch* to Vermeer's *The Milkmaid*, the Dutch Golden Age is shown in all its splendour.
📷 *Tip: Danish artist Jeppe Hein's water pavilion sits in the museum garden. Once you're there, you have about 12 seconds to get to the middle and take a picture before you get very wet.*

➤ p. 52, Sightseeing

VAN GOGH MUSEUM ⭐2

The biggest collection of Van Gogh's paintings in the world, proving there is more to him than just sunflowers!

➤ p. 52, Sightseeing

TUSCHINSKI ⭐5

Beatrix, the former Queen, has been known to go to this expressionist cinema.

📷 *Tip: In the upper circle you can get up close to the stunning ceiling decoration.*

➤ p. 93, Going out

CONCERTGEBOUW ⭐8

Have a listen! A venerable old concert hall with famously good acoustics.

➤ p. 96, Going out

JORDAAN ⭐7

Quaint houses, ancient bars and loads of well-hidden *hofjes* make this former working-class district one of Amsterdam's most charming neighbourhoods.

➤ p. 39, Sightseeing

KONINGSDAG ⭐10

On King's Day, the whole of Amsterdam goes slightly crazy, kicking things off with a city-wide flea market before enjoying beer and Oranjebitte liqueur.

➤ p. 102, Active & relaxed

CONTENTS

⏱	Plan your visit	🍴	Eating/drinking	☂	Rainy day activities
€–€€€	Price categories	🛍	Shopping	🐷	Budget activities
(*)	Premium-rate phone number	🍸	Going out	👯	Family activities
		🌴	Top beaches	🚩	Classic experiences

(📖 A2) Refers to the removable pull-out map
(0) Located off the map

CONTENTS

BEST OF
AMSTERDAM

Bicycles speed across the bridge at the junction of Keizers- and Leidsegracht

BEST ☂ WHEN IT RAINS

ACTIVITIES TO BRIGHTEN YOUR DAY

A LIBRARY FOR THE 21ST CENTURY

The *Centrale OBA* (library; photo) offers more than just dusty old books. You can admire the trendy furniture made by Dutch designers, surf the internet, listen to music, leaf through a newspaper or have a coffee.
➤ p. 32, Sightseeing

FROM CITY HALL TO PALACE

King Willem-Alexander rarely stays in the *Koninklijk Paleis*, which was origi- nally built as a city hall. Nonetheless, its impressive rooms are well worth seeing, especially the Great Hall, which depicts the universe with Amsterdam at its centre.
➤ p. 35, Sightseeing

EYE TO EYE WITH THE STARS

You can spend a whole afternoon at the *Eye Film Institute*, flitting between its exhibitions, café and shop. If the rain persists, you can work your way through a huge film archive in the yellow viewing pods in the permanent exhibition.
➤ p. 54, Sightseeing

SHOPPING IN THE POST OFFICE

The *Magna Plaza* shopping centre was built as the city's main post office in the 19th century. Today, this imposing Gothic Revival building houses upmarket shops and cafés in its spacious courtyard.
➤ p. 74, Shopping

COSY CINEMA

The Movies on Haarlemmerdijk is Amsterdam's oldest cinema and has retained its Art Deco style. After the film, stay for a beer in the cosy cinema pub.
➤ p. 93, Going out

BEST

ON A BUDGET

FOR SMALLER WALLETS

A TEMPLE TO COLOUR
With beautifully ornate decoration, the Buddhist *Fo Guang Shan He Hua Temple* is nestled between traditional brick buildings on the Zeedjik, where it serves as the religious heart of Amsterdam's Chinatown.
➤ p. 34, Sightseeing

GALLERIES IN JORDAAN
Contemporary art does not need to be exclusive. A wander through Amsterdam's galleries gives you a chance to look without buying. Most of the most famous galleries, such as *Fons Welters*, *Annet Gelink* and *Torch*, are situated close together in the Jordaan district.
➤ p. 39, Sightseeing & p. 83, Shopping

PARK LIFE
Vondelpark is Amsterdam's place to meet in summer, whether it's to listen to one of the many free open-air concerts, have a picnic or play football. This park is a magnet for social gatherings rather than a place for peace and quiet (photo).
➤ p. 50, Sightseeing

MIDDAY CLASSICS
The lunchtime concerts in the *Concertgebouw* are an Amsterdam institution – and they are free. The Concertgebouw Orchestra rehearses every Wednesday at 12.30pm, and there are also occasional concerts by young prodigies.
➤ p. 96, Going out

OPEN-AIR CINEMA
The *Pluk de Nacht* outdoor film festival runs over several weeks in August and is held on a small peninsula on Westerdoksdijk. You only have to pay if you want a warm blanket to go with your deckchair.
➤ p. 103, Going out

BEST WITH CHILDREN

FUN FOR YOUNG & OLD

CLIMB ABOARD A CANAL BOAT

What does a houseboat actually look like inside? The *Houseboat Museum* on the Prinsengracht has all the answers. The *Hendrika Maria* was built as a cargo ship but is now open to visitors.

➤ p. 40, Sightseeing

HANDS-ON SCIENCE

The *NEMO Science Museum* (photo) houses a huge interactive exhibition on scientific phenomena. The highlight is the massive chain reaction, which is set off once per hour.

➤ p. 45, Sightseeing

ANIMAL MAGIC

Amsterdam's *ARTIS* zoo is a little gem. The butterfly house, where insects buzz around you, is wonderful. The lemur island and seal-feeding displays more than justify the ticket price.

➤ p. 46, Sightseeing

BACTERIA, VIRUSES & FUNGI

They're everywhere – on our skin, in our mouths, on our feet and, of course, in our stomachs. *Micropia* explains everything there is to know about the tiny organisms all over our bodies.

➤ p. 46, Sightseeing

PANCAKES AHOY!

Combine a harbour tour with a plate of pancakes for a real crowd-pleaser. The kids will also get an extra surprise when a hatch on the *Pannenkoekenboot* opens to reveal a huge ball pit.

➤ p. 72, Eating & drinking

PEDAL POWER

If you want to do more than just look at the Grachten, you can hire pedalos from *Stromma*. Beware, though – charting a course between the tourist boats won't be easy. Ponchos are provided if it rains.

➤ p. 100, Active & relaxed

BEST ⚑
CLASSIC EXPERIENCES

CANALSIDE LIVING

The houses on Amsterdam's canals can be quaintly crooked, or imposing and elegant. Lining the canals of the old town, they may all be brick-built but when you look more closely, no two are alike. The grandest residences are in the *Gouden Bocht* (golden arc) on the Herengracht.
➤ p. 42, Sightseeing

BRIDGES AS FAR AS THE EYE CAN SEE

In the old town alone there are no less than 600 bridges, the most famous of which is the *Magere Brug* (photo) which crosses the Amstel. The Oudezijds Achterburgwal is now home to the world's first *3D-printed bridge*.
➤ p. 44, Sightseeing

BROWN CAFÉS

The wood-panelled "brown cafés" that you find on almost every street corner in Amsterdam are always cosy and sociable. Some of these special pubs, such as *De Oosterling* or *Wynand Fockink*, are several hundred years old.
➤ p. 92, Going out

A PARTY FIT FOR A KING

On 27 April, everyone in the Netherlands celebrates King Willem-Alexander. The day begins with a city-wide flea market which then turns into a street party in the afternoon. Paint yourself (and the town) orange!
➤ p. 102, Active & relaxed

CYCLE CITY

Would Amsterdam be the same city without the bikes? There are rental companies everywhere so you can blend in. *Star Bikes Rental* is particularly friendly, and they make a decent coffee, too.
➤ p. 130, Good to know

GET TO KNOW AMSTERDAM

No glistening chrome, no high tech – a proper Amsterdam *fiets* is decorated with rust and flowers

DISCOVER AMSTERDAM

Experience open-air "gezellig" at the beach bar on the site of the former NDSM shipyard

Crooked, slim houses lean on each other for support, a cyclist crosses a bridge on a squeaking bike, and people sit outside cafés having a beer. In the distance you can hear a tram rumbling across the Leidseplein. There is no doubt that Amsterdam is a charming city. It captivates millions of visitors every year with its relaxed, lively atmosphere, and just about everyone immediately feels at home.

POCKET-SIZED METROPOLIS
One secret of its success is that, because Amsterdam is an incredibly diverse city, it can lay claim to being the world's smallest metropolis. Old and new, calm and bustling, hipster and commercial, provincial and cosmopolitan, individual and

1275
Amsterdam granted tax privileges by Count Floris V; the first record of the city's name

1602
Founding of the Dutch East India Company

1612
Start of construction of the Canal Ring

1876
The opening of the North Sea Canal industrialises the city

25–26 February 1941
Strike in protest against the persecution of the Jewish population

5 May 1945
Liberation from German occupation

on-trend – this is a city of rich contradictions. The city's almost 8,500 listed buildings mean Amsterdam has more architectural gems than any other Dutch city.

ANCIENT CITY, YOUNG POPULATION

Thanks to its compact centre, you will probably explore most of the city, which is built on 90 islands, on foot. Only by walking the cobbled streets along the canals can you take in the elegance of the tall, narrow-fronted merchants' houses, spot a heron on the roof of a houseboat, or discover one of the hidden *hofje* (courtyards) or a cool little boutique. The architecture on the Canal Ring has not been altered in centuries. For this reason, the area was given UNESCO World Heritage status in 2010. The fact that Amsterdam has not become a lifeless theme park, but instead remains a vibrant city, is thanks to the relaxed attitude of the Dutch when it comes to their historic buildings – they are unafraid to do things like putting a neon sign on a Gothic church – but it also stems in part from the city's exceptionally cosmopolitan and young population. Half of Amsterdam's residents were not born in the Netherlands, and 41 per cent of them are under 35 years old. This is what gives the nightlife around Leidseplein and Rembrandtplein such a buzz. It also accounts for the almost unlimited range of shops in the city and the abundance of cafés, bars and restaurants that makes it hard to decide where to go.

1970
Camping in Vondelpark – popular with hippies and backpackers – is banned

1996
The first Canal Parade, now part of Amsterdam Pride

2 February 2002
Crown Prince Willem-Alexander marries Argentinian Máxima Zorreguieta in the Nieuwe Kerk

2010
The Canal Ring is declared a UNESCO World Heritage site

2019
Amsterdam's tourist board gives up marketing the city after a record 21 million tourists visit the city in 2018

POPULAR WITH PASSING TOURISTS

Amsterdam is nice at any time of the year – in summer, when the cafés put tables out on the street and an almost Mediterranean atmosphere prevails, or in winter, when the canals are veiled in mist and the bridges are decked in lights. The city's boat companies have not missed this trick, and organise the December *Amsterdam Light Festival*, with tours through the beautifully illuminated old town. Nobody should skip the city's three major museums, the Rijksmuseum, Van Gogh Museum and Stedelijk Museum, with their stunning collections, or the hundreds of interesting shops in the city centre. The popularity of Amsterdam as a destination for visitors from all over the world is largely due to the relaxed and unshowy nature of its people. These days the city gets around 21 million visitors a year; as a result, it can get very crowded – especially in popular spots. To keep tourism in check, Airbnb is strictly regulated and hotel construction has been temporarily stopped, and museums increasingly require advance booking.

INSIDER TIP
Seeing old canals in a new light

FROM A FISHING VILLAGE TO A TRADING CENTRE

The city's history has been largely shaped by its tolerance and global perspective. It originated as a marshy fishing village at the point where the river Amstel flowed into the IJsselmeer, which is today a lake but was then part of the North Sea. In 1275, the village of Amstelledamme was granted freedom from customs duties and a town charter followed in 1300. From then onwards, the town controlled the flow of goods between the North Sea and the Dutch hinterland. The commercially minded Amsterdammers were always on the lookout for new opportunities, and it was not long before they were trading across the Baltic and North Sea regions. To protect themselves against high tides, they started to construct a line of defences, *de Wallen*. The oldest quarter of the city between Oudezijds and Nieuwezijds Achterburgwal, which has been well preserved for the most part, is now Chinatown and the red-light district.

THE GOLDEN AGE

At the end of the 16th century, the northern Netherlands gained independence from Spanish rule in the 80 Years' War. Word spread quickly, and the area soon attracted many Protestant and Jewish refugees from places like Antwerp and Lisbon that were still ruled by Spain. The influx of wealthy merchants among these immigrants extended trade connections, which ushered in the Dutch Golden Age. In 1602, the Dutch East India Company (Verenigde Oostindische Compagnie – VOC) was founded to trade with the Far East and India; and, in 1621, the Westindische Compagnie was founded to carry out trade with America and the west coast of Africa. Over the next 150 years, the Netherlands became one of the leading European naval and commercial powers. Amsterdam grew to be a rich and important port, with warehouses full of cloves, cinnamon, silk, coffee and porcelain. Within a few decades, the number of residents increased five-fold.

FINE ART & CANALSIDE LIVING

In the early 17th century, with the city bursting at the seams, construction was started on a series of concentric rings of canals. Outside the old *Wallen*, rich merchants built fine residences with attached warehouses on Herengracht, Keizersgracht or Prinsengracht. And these impressive houses naturally had to be filled with the finest things, which in turn led to the Golden Age of Dutch art. The greatest works from this period, such as Rembrandt's *The Night Watch* and Vermeer's *The Milkmaid,* can be admired in the Rijksmuseum today. Around 1700, Amsterdam had a population of about 220,000, making it the third-largest city in Europe, and it had reached the peak of its prosperity. Just 50 years later, the Netherlands' star had begun to fade as other countries took over as rulers of the seas. The economy began to recover in the mid-19th century thanks to industrialisation and the construction of the Nordzeekanal, which enabled ocean-going ships to enter the port of Amsterdam.

JUST FIVE DAYS OF WAR

During World War Two, the Netherlands fell to German forces after five days of fighting. The speed of the capitulation meant that Amsterdam suffered little

The large *Schiffartsmuseum* is a reminder of former Dutch sea power

damage, preserving the city's historic architecture. There was resistance to the German occupation, but it was unable to prevent the almost complete annihilation of the city's Jewish community – Anne Frank among them.

AMSTERDAM: HIPPY CENTRAL

In the 1970s, Amsterdam became a magnet for hippies, squatters and drop-outs from all over the world. Although it is hard to imagine today, thousands of backpackers camped out in Vondelpark and on the Dam in summer, and by 1980 there were around 20,000 squatters in the city. Liberal politicians pushed through the legalisation of soft drugs, and Amsterdam is still renowned for its liberal politics. It is not just tulips and canals that make up the city's image, but also "coffee shops" and the red-light district.

CONSERVATISM IS ON THE RISE

Things are changing though, and local policies have become much more conservative in recent years. Squatting has been illegal since the end of 2010, and coffee shops in suburban areas are only permitted to serve Dutch residents. But Amsterdam still dances to its own tune. Despite growing criticism from some in the city about ineffective integration and high unemployment rates among the Moroccan and Turkish immigrant populations, the city council still leans to the left and Amsterdam's coffee shops are open to all comers.

BUILDING FRENZY ON THE IJ

Today, you increasingly see cranes and building sites across the city. A lot has happened in recent years, especially on the banks of the IJ. Completely new quarters of the city have risen up in the former dockland area to the east of the main station, and construction work around the new *Eye Film Institute* on the north bank and in the old timber docks to the west of the inner city is still in progress. Amsterdammers are not fans of stasis, which is why a lot of city life is moving out of the city centre into the former residential and harbour districts on its outskirts.In the historic centre, much of this still goes unnoticed. Amsterdam is and will remain a compact, remarkably laid-back, sometimes rather chaotic metropolis with about 860,000 inhabitants. Their preferred means of transport is an often-rusty but eco-friendly *fiets* (bicycle). Cafés are an important part of life in the city. Whether dingy pubs, trendy bars or vegan eateries, what matters is that they are "gezellig" – cosy and sociable.

AMSTERDAM HAS SOMETHING FOR EVERYONE

Thanks to its enormous diversity, Amsterdam attracts many kinds of visitors. But when the elms are reflected in the water of the canals and the glockenspiel of the Westerkerk chimes in the background, they all fall for its charms.

AT A GLANCE

864,000
Population

Leeds: 793,000

21 MILLION
Tourists per year
Population of the Netherlands:
17 million

1,539
Bridges

Venice: 435 bridges

167
Nationalities

New York: 193

LOWEST POINT IN THE CITY:

WATERGRAAFSMEER-POLDER
6.7M
Below sea level

DAYS OF RAIN PER YEAR

185
London: 156

165 CANALS WITH

2,500
HOUSEBOATS

Every house in Amsterdam is held up by wooden piles – 10 on average.
But the Concertgebouw sits on a remarkable 2,000,
Centraal Station on around 9,000
and the Koninklijk Paleis on over 13,000.

207
Vincent van Gogh
paintings

FAMOUS FOOTBALLERS
Johan Cruyff
Marco Van Basten

**25,000 BIKES
END UP IN THE
CANALS EACH YEAR**

UNDERSTAND AMSTERDAM

BICYCLES

There are around 880,000 bicycles in Amsterdam, which is more than the city's population. Every day, 53% of people over twelve years old use a bike – in a compact but permanently congested city with few parking spaces and delivery vans everywhere, a *fiets* is the best way to get about. Cyclists are allowed to do almost anything, including riding side by side and carrying passengers on their racks. That said, lights are a must and the police regularly run checks in the evenings. Most bikes in the city are in an awful condition – a deliberate and smart tactic against theft.

DUTCH DESIGN

All over the world, simple but quirky products by Dutch designers are in high demand. It all started with *Droog Design* ("dry design"), a collective of young designers who got together in the mid-1990s with plans to revolutionise the super smooth design world. In no time at all, their first products – including an armchair made from old clothing and a chandelier from a bunch of lightbulbs – became world-famous. Since then, Dutch design has almost become a brand of its own, and Droog Design has opened a popular store-cum-gallery in Staalstraat selling cool products by young designers. The most internationally successful Droog alumnus, Marcel Wanders, has taken a different path, opting to experiment with a neo-Baroque style – although his tongue is firmly in his cheek. Since 2009, an old school in Jordaan has been home to his design label *Moooi*. This move was made possible by the city council, which has actively supported the design sector in recent years. The city also paid to furnish the public library (*Centrale OBA*, see p. 32) with Dutch designer pieces, and has promoted the establishment of studios in former brothels in the red-light district. These endeavours speak volumes about the way Amsterdam would like to develop as a tourist destination.

THREE MAYORS

Every city needs a mayor, but not every city has three! It is no surprise that this bike-mad, party city also has a cycling and night mayor alongside the usual one. The night mayor represents the interests of Amsterdam's nightlife, acting as a mediator between the city, residents and the clubbing industry. In 2014, he pushed through 24-hour licences for some clubs.

The office of the bicycle mayor was created in 2016, since when it has been held by Anna Luten, the "voice of cyclists at city hall". Her job is to take care of improving the city's bike paths and parking while advocating for the interests of cyclists – although some visitors might not think this is really necessary in Amsterdam …

OPEN THE LOCKS!

Amsterdam is known as the "Venice of the North". This nickname comes from the many *grachten*, or canals, that course around the historic city centre. The canals once functioned as sewers. Once a day, the sluice gates were opened and dirty water flowed out into the Zuiderzee (today the Ijsselmeer). Nowadays, the water is still circulated several times a week. In the 1960s and 1970s, several canals were filled in to create roads. Only their names – Vijzelgracht, Lindengracht, Palmgracht – reveal that these streets were once waterways.

HOME ON THE WATER

Some look like posh homes, others little more than shabby wrecks; some

Amsterdammers make their homes on land and water

The royal couple and their children greet the crowds on Koningsdag

are refurbished freight boats, whereas others are modern and purposebuilt. The city canals, especially Singel and Prinsengracht, host 2,500 houseboats. Students in the 1950s first hit on the idea that disused boats would make excellent places to live. They are now home to eccentrics and people who have fallen in love with a life on the water. However, the city has opposed the profusion of houseboats and rarely issues mooring permits today.

THE IJ

A large stretch of water behind the main station, the *IJ* (pronounced "eye") forms the northern border of Amsterdam's inner city. It is hard to say exactly what the IJ is. A river? An estuary? A lake? None of these descriptions really nail it. Before 1932,

when the Enclosure Dam in the north of Holland was built, the IJsselmeer to the east of Amsterdam was still called the Zuiderzee and was part of the North Sea with the IJ one of its larger bays. It was once enclosed to the west by large dunes before a canal opened it up to the rest of the North Sea in 1876. At the same time, a dam and the Oranje sluices were built in the north of Amsterdam to separate the IJ from the IJsselmeer. Despite its salty water and the fact that sea fish feel absolutely at home in it, the IJ is usually described as a river today.

BEATRIX & CO

The Netherlands is a constitutional monarchy. However, this has not always been the case. Although the house of Orange-Nassau has ruled since 1572, Holland was initially a republic after the wars of liberation against Spain. For some 200 years, the Orange rulers were only governors. The first king, Willem I, did not ascend the throne until 1815, following the withdrawal of Napoleon's forces.

It may seem surprising that the pragmatic Dutch still allow themselves the luxury of a royal family. But just like her mother Juliana, who died in 2004 and was known to be particularly close to her people, Queen Beatrix (b. 1938), who succeeded to the throne in 1980 and abdicated in 2013, is very popular. Her role as the darling of the Dutch people has now been taken by her daughter-in-law, Máxima (b. 1971), who steals the show when she makes public appearances with her husband, King Willem-Alexander (b. 1967). Always clad in stylish designer clothes, this Argentinean commoner knows how to charm. Whenever the royal couple and their three daughters Amalia (b. 2003), Alexia (b. 2005) and Ariane (b. 2007) make an appearance on TV, the viewing figures spike.

HOT & CRISPY

Deep fried and deliciously unhealthy, *kroket*, *frikandel*, *loempia* and *patat oorlog* are the stars of Amsterdam's snacking scene. Some of these reveal gastronomic influences from the country's colonial past, like *loempia* (a cigar-shaped spring roll with sweet chilli sauce), *bamischijf* (deep-fried discs of spicy noodles) and *patat oorlog* (fries with mayonnaise, peanut

TRUE OR FALSE?

AMSTERDAM IS A STONER PARADISE

Many people's image of Amsterdam involves drugs being legally sold on every corner. But this stereotype is misleading: drugs are not legal in the Netherlands, they are just tolerated ("gedogen" in Dutch). The truth is that they are strictly regulated. You can only buy up to 5g of cannabis in special coffee shops, and the number of these shops has almost halved from a peak of 300 in 1999 to around 160 today. However, seek and you will definitely find.

ALL THE HOUSES IN AMSTERDAM ARE THIN

Space has long been at a premium in Amsterdam, as the city's many thin houses attest. Oude Hoogstraat 22 holds the record, at just under 2.02m in width. The house at Kloveniersburgwal 26 is not much wider at 2.44m. This was originally built for the wealthy Trip family's coachman – the Trip family lived directly opposite in the widest house in the Old Town (22m). The coachman is said to have wished "if only I had a house as wide as the front door of my master's", and to this day his old abode bears witness to the fact that dreams can come true.

What will they think of next? An automatic snack dispenser for canal boats

sauce and onions). But *nieuwe haring* (lightly salted herring) is both a popular snack and as Dutch as you can get – they are best bought from street stalls.

The zenith of Amsterdam's snack culture is the so-called *automatiek*, a vending machine for hot and greasy foods. Behind little doors, cheese soufflés, meatballs and croquettes wait for someone to throw a few euros into the slot, open the door and devour them. The best-known *automatiek* chain is called *Febo*. It was founded in 1941 and can be found on almost every corner in Amsterdam. But connoisseurs swear by the home-made shrimp and meat croquettes from Holtkamp Bakery at 15 Vijzelgracht, which can also be found on the menus of some restaurants.

INSIDER TIP
Crispy croquettes

HEAVE-HO!

Virtually every house, irrespective of age, has a hoist beam with a hook, which usually sticks out above a window in the roof. It comes as a surprise to many to learn that they are still used today. The stairs in Amsterdam's houses are extremely steep and narrow, which makes it almost impossible to take larger items to the upper floors. So residents hire a pulley from a removal company, attach it to the beam to hoist up wardrobes, pianos and anything else that is bulky, and haul them in through a window.

XXX

No matter where you are in the city, you are likely to see the symbol of three crosses. It adorns not only the crown on the top of the Westertoren, but also the gables of canal-side houses and the little brown posts known as *Amsterdammertjes* that separate the pavement from the road in the city centre. Some visitors speculate that they have something to do with the red-light district and X-rated films – and in many shops you can buy humorous souvenirs that play on this association. However, in reality they are the three St Andrew's crosses, which have been part of the city coat of arms since the Middle Ages. It is not clear why the coat of arms features these crosses. It may be connected to the fact that most Amsterdammers were once fishermen like St Andrew. Beginning in 1505, all ships registered in Amsterdam were required to fly the flag with the three crosses.

CURTAIN-FREE!

There are remarkably few curtains in Amsterdam. This is as true in people's houses as in the red-tinted windows of the red-light district. People might tell you this is because of a historical "curtain tax" which put the miserly Amsterdammers off having any kind of window draperies. However, this is a myth – there was a window tax in the 19th century but this had no impact on curtains or blinds.

It is more likely that the grand houses on the canals never needed curtains. Their smartest reception room looks over the street and it may have been a status symbol to let people look in. Behind this room is a private living room which is not on public view. Some people think the Calvinist religion is the real reason: a good Calvinist has nothing to hide, and so lets people look into their home. The expensive designer furniture in many of these houses today suggests that showing off may provide the more plausible explanation. In theory, though, good Dutch Calvinists would never look into someone else's house, no matter how easy it is.

Amsterdam's coat of arms

SIGHT SEEING

Amsterdam has no fewer than 8,500 listed buildings. Most of them are situated within comfortable walking distance of the city centre – either in De Wallen, the oldest district of the city, or on the Canal Ring.

Nobody should leave Amsterdam without taking a proper walk along Singel, Herengracht, Keizersgracht or Prinsengracht. And some of the newer or lesser-known quarters of the city are also worth a detour. Take the free ferry on the northern edge of the IJ or a

The green NEMO building emerges from the harbour like an inquisitive whale

walk through Albert Cuyp market to see other sides of this vibrant, pulsating city.

If you have come to explore the rich history of Dutch art, the country's three most important museums (the Rijksmuseum, Van Gogh Museum and Stedelijk Museum) are conveniently situated in one square: the Museumplein. Amsterdam's museums are not only for art lovers – if you're into handbags, houseboats or hippy

NEIGHBOURHOOD OVERVIEW

GRACHTENRING & JORDAAN p. 39
Go back to the Golden Age

OUD ZUID & DE PIJP p. 49
Amsterdam high society meets urban street market

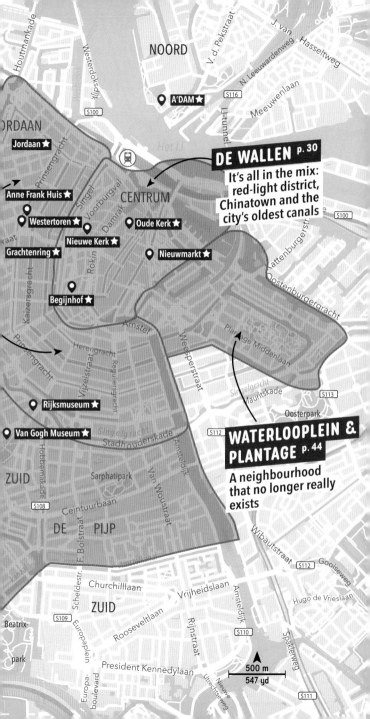

NOORD

A'DAM ★

DE WALLEN p. 30

It's all in the mix: red-light district, Chinatown and the city's oldest canals

JORDAAN

Jordaan ★

Anne Frank Huis ★

CENTRUM

Westertoren ★

Nieuwe Kerk ★

Oude Kerk ★

Grachtenring ★

Nieuwmarkt ★

Begijnhof ★

Rijksmuseum ★

Plantage Middenlaan

Van Gogh Museum ★

Oosterpark

WATERLOOPLEIN & PLANTAGE p. 44

A neighbourhood that no longer really exists

ZUID

Sarphatipark

DE PIJP

ZUID

Beatrix park

500 m
547 yd

If you plan to visit a few museums, it's worth buying a *Museumkaart (MK | museumkaart.nl)*. This annual pass gets you into most major Dutch museums. For adults, it costs 64.90 euros and for under-18s it is 32.45 euros. You will begin to make savings after about the fourth museum you visit (and passholders don't have to queue). The pass is sold at every museum and can be used straight away. Museums that accept the *Museumkaart* are marked in this travel guide with the letters MK in brackets next to the admission price.

DE WALLEN

Amsterdam's medieval centre De Wallen takes its name from the four oldest canals in the city: defensive moats called Voorburgwal and Achterburgwal, which surrounded the "oude" and "nieuwe zijde" (the "old" and "new side" of the city).

Only two of these canals still exist because those on the "new side" were filled in. Around the two remaining canals, one of the most vibrant and edgy neighbourhoods has grown up and includes the red-light district and Chinatown. Here you will find Amsterdam's oldest church and best Asian food stalls but also its grungiest corners. This makes for a diverse mix of people: tourists, junkies, old-school Amsterdammers, prostitutes and students go about their business between neon signs and canalside houses. The buildings look much less

WHERE TO START?

Dam (⌘ F3) is the ideal starting point for exploring Amsterdam. This historic city square on the street running from the main station is the site of the Nationaal Monument, the Royal Palace and the Nieuwe Kerk, and also the long-established department store Bijenkorf. It also marks the start of the Kalverstraat shopping street. You can park a car at Bijenkorf but it is cheaper and less stressful to walk five minutes from the station or take a tram: lines 1, 2, 4, 5, 9, 11, 12 13, 14, 17 and 24 stop at the Dam. Rokin metro station (line 52) is also close by.

smart here than on the upmarket Canal Ring. The houses were built between the 14th and 16th centuries when there were no strict regulations. As a result they are wonderfully diverse in size and style. Take a quick break to look at their façades or duck into the Begijnhof to escape the frenzy of Kalverstraat.

1 CENTRAAL STATION

The grand main station was built in 1889 in neo-Renaissance style by Petrus JH Cuypers, the architect of the Rijksmuseum. This "Travellers' Palace" is supported by more than 10,000 tree trunks that were rammed into the sandy soil. The station has been redesigned several times since then and has gradually expanded. Go through its shopping arcades to get to the new

DE WALLEN

1 Centraal Station | S100 |
3 Schreierstoren
Centrale OBA
2
Ons' Lieve
Heer op Solder
10
4 Scheepvaarthuis
Beurs van Berlage **11**
Nieuwe Kerk ★
9 **Oude Kerk ★**
8 Chinatown
15
Koninklijk
Paleis **14**
12 Nationaal Monument
13 Madame Tussauds
7 De Waag
6 **Nieuwmarkt ★**
5 Montelbaanstoren
16 Amsterdam Dungeon
17 Amsterdam Museum
18 **Begijnhof ★**
19 Spui
20 Munttoren
Hortus
Botanicus
300 m
328 yd

concourse on its north side which has restaurants with everything from

INSIDER TIP
Delft tiles in the bike tunnel

sushi to burgers and a great sea view. Check out the bike tunnel at the western end of the station – it's decorated with a tiled mural depicting sailing boats, designed by Irma Boom.

This artwork caused quite a stir when it was unveiled because a ship from the rival city of Rotterdam is depicted front and centre. Free ferries depart for Amsterdam-Noord from the rear side of the station. *The main station is the central terminus for trams, buses, boat tours & museum boats* | 🔲 G3

✷ CENTRALE OBA ☂

Amsterdam's public library is a real magnet for visitors. This impressive new building on Oosterdok island is entirely furnished with the work of Dutch designers. On the top floor there is a good canteen with a terrace that offers a wonderful view of the historic city centre. *Mon–Fri 8am–10pm, Sat/Sun 10am–10pm | Oosterdokskade 143 | 5 min walk from the main station |* ⧠ *H3*

✸ SCHREIERSTOREN

On the battlements of this semicircular defensive tower built in 1484, sailors' wives supposedly wept as ships departed. Although a 17th-century gable stone tells this story, it is not true.

The tower was originally called *schreyhoekstoren* because it sits where two canals meet at a sharp angle *(schreye hoek)*. Henry Hudson sailed from here – the subject of many paintings – to North America in 1609, where he discovered Manhattan and founded New Amsterdam, later known as New York. The Hudson River and Hudson Bay are named after him. The tower houses a cosy café. *Prins Hendrikkade 94–95 | 5 min walk from the main station |* ⧠ *G3*

✹ SCHEEPVAARTHUIS

At first sight, the "house of seafaring" looks like the setting for a Batman film. Forbidding and even a little threatening, it stands on Binnenkade to the east of the main station. It was built in

Like a Gotham City film set: the Van der Mey Hall in the Scheepvaarthuis

1916 and is an early example of Brick Expressionism, which became famous as the "Amsterdam School". Originally the headquarters of large shipping companies, it has housed the *Grand Hotel Amrâth* since 2007. Even if you're not staying here, have a look at the grand staircase with its wrought iron decoration and elaborate glass roof. *Prins Hendrikkade 108–114 | 5 min walk from the main station | ◫ H3*

5 MONTELBAANSTOREN

This little tower is one of the most popular things to photograph in town. It was built in the 16th century as part of the defences on the Oude Schans canal – which was then the city's outer limit. Legend has it that the bells once began to peal at odd times, earning the tower its nickname, "Malle Jaap" ("Crazy Jacob"). Since 1878 Amsterdam's waterworks have used the tower to monitor the water level and circulation in the canals. *Oudeschans 2 | metro 51, 53, 54 Nieuwmarkt | ◫ H4*

6 NIEUWMARKT ★

The bar- and café-lined Nieuwmarkt sits between Chinatown and the red-light district with the old weigh house at its centre. It is a great place to while away an hour people-watching. During the day the market stalls are full of life, but at night the crowds throng towards the red-light district. On a sunny summer's day, Nieuwmarkt is the perfect place to catch a few last rays with a glass of wine at sunset. *Metro 51, 53, 54 Nieuwmarkt | ◫ G4*

7 DE WAAG

Amsterdam's oldest secular building stands in the middle of Nieuwmarkt. Today, the former weigh house is home to an institute for contemporary media and a café, but it was built in 1488 as a city gate and converted into a weigh house when the Canal Ring was constructed in the 17th century. All Dutch cities had a weigh house where merchants could weigh cheese and other goods to make sure that there was no swindling going on. In the attic, the guild of surgeons installed a so-called Anatomical Theatre, which has been preserved and can be viewed during events held by the media institute. At one of the many public dissections that took place in the *Anatomical Theatre*, Rembrandt painted his famous *Anatomy Lesson of Dr Tulp* (1632), which now hangs in The Hague in the Het Mauritshuis museum. *Metro 51, 53, 54 Nieuwmarkt | ◫ G4*

8 CHINATOWN

Amsterdam's Chinatown is located around the Zeedijk and the Nieuwmarkt. In the early 20th century many Chinese sailors came to the city. Some stayed and brought their families to join them. The Chinese still form a close-knit community and keep up their cultural traditions. In Chinatown there are lots of authentic Chinese restaurants with Peking ducks dangling in their windows, as

The local community celebrates traditional festivals in Chinatown's narrow streets

well as Chinese bakeries, boutiques and medical practices. The colourful icing on the cake is the Buddhist *Fo Guang Shan He Hua Temple (Tue–Sat noon–5pm, Sun 10am–5pm | Zeedijk 106–118 | metro 51, 53, 54 Nieuwmarkt),* which is open to the public with free admission. *G3*

9 OUDE KERK ★

Built around 1300, Amsterdam's oldest church sits in the middle of the red-light district today. It is tightly wedged between the surrounding houses, and the eclectic mix of goings-on that take place inside them sum up Amsterdam pretty well: hipsters sip their soy lattes next to red-lit windows showcasing scantily dressed women while kids play in a nearby garden. The church is a patchwork of different architectural styles and has been extensively redesigned. Several chapels were added in the 15th century, followed by works to make the whole building taller in the 16th century. Nowadays, concerts and modern art exhibitions are held here. *Mon–Sat 10am–6pm, Sun 1–5pm | admission 10 euros (MK) | Oudekerksplein 23 | oudekerk.nl | tram 4, 9, 16, 24 Damrak | G3*

10 ONS' LIEVE HEER OP SOLDER

Nothing on the outside of this old house on the canal in the red-light district betrays what is hidden inside. On the lower floors it appears to be a normal 17th-century merchant's home and exploring it gives you a sense of a merchant's life in the Golden Age. But the main attraction is hidden away in the attic: a three-storey secret Catholic church, built in 1661, containing a high altar and two galleries. As the ruling Calvinists had prohibited Catholics from practising their religion openly, worshippers had to sneak into the house by a side entrance. *Mon–Sat 10am–6pm, Sun 1–6pm | admission 11 euros (MK) | Oudezijds Voorburgwal 38 | opsolder.nl | tram 4, 14, 24 Dam | ⊞ G3*

⑪ BEURS VAN BERLAGE

With its tower visible from a distance, this brick building presides like a castle over the Damrak. The stock exchange, built 1897–1903 to plans made by the architect Hendrik Petrus Berlage, is regarded as a cornerstone of modernist architecture in the Netherlands, thanks to its plain façade and openly visible structural elements.

Initially the owners were not at all pleased with the building. They would have preferred a grand neo-Renaissance building like the Rijksmuseum or the main station. However, Berlage specifically wanted to move away from this style. He invited some of his artist friends to decorate the building with contemporary ornamentation and works of art. Murals, sculptures, decorative ironwork and aphorisms complement the massive architecture to create a unique piece of art. The building can only be visited during exhibitions and events but you can get a sense of its magnificence in *Bistro Berlage (daily | bistroberlage.nl)*.

On the other side of the street, be sure to take a look at the *Beurspassage*. Designed by artist duo Arno Coenen and Iris Roskam, the decoration appears to be old. But a closer look reveals the chandelier is made from old bikes and the lights are made to look like ice-cream cones. *beursvanberlage.nl | tram 4, 14, 24 Dam | ⊞ G3*

INSIDER TIP Appearances can deceive

⑫ NATIONAAL MONUMENT

The national monument is opposite the palace on the Dam. This 22-m-high obelisk, inaugurated in 1956, commemorates the victims of German occupation and is a monument to liberation and peace. In 1995 there was a minor scandal when it needed restoration and the only firm able to carry out the work turned out to be German. *Tram 4, 14, 24 Dam | ⊞ F3*

⑬ MADAME TUSSAUD'S

If you always wanted to stand next to Rembrandt, Kylie Minogue or King Willem-Alexander and are prepared to pay a lot of money for the privilege, you can almost make your dream come true here. Wax sculptures of celebrities from all walks of life, some of them more real-looking than others. *Daily 10am–7pm | admission 24.50 euros | Dam 20 | tram 2, 4, 11, 12, 13, 14, 17, 24 Dam | ◷ 1 hr | ⊞ F3*

⑭ KONINKLIJK PALEIS ⚲

At first sight, the plain grey building on the Dam with its curtained windows does not look very regal and sometimes it is rather disrespectfully referred to as "Holland's biggest broom cupboard". Indeed, it was built as a city hall, not a royal palace. Jacob van Campen was the architect of this Renaissance building, erected 1648–1655. To support the weight of the imposing sandstone, 13,659 piles had to be driven into the ground. A huge frieze depicting all kinds of sea monsters adorns the main façade. On the inside, the huge and elaborately decorated central hall is the main attraction. In more sombre mode, the smaller (but no less impressive) Vierschaar is a court where death sentences were once handed down. The city hall only became a palace in 1930. The main residence of the House of Orange is in The Hague – the King only stays in his Amsterdam palace for receptions, and it is not open to the public when he is in residence. For up-to-date opening times, see *paleisamsterdam.nl* or *tel. 020 6 20 40 60* | *admission 10 euros (MK)* | *tram 1, 2, 4, 5, 9, 13, 14, 16, 17, 24 Dam* | ⏱ *1 hr* | 🗺 *F3*

🔢 NIEUWE KERK ★

The imposing gothic Nieuwe Kerk on the Dam is Amsterdam's most famous church. However, it is not as new as its name suggests. Construction began in the 15th century, when the city had outgrown its first set of fortifications and the Oude Kerk had become too small. The church gained its present form around 1540 after several fires and renovations. Just 38 years later, during a campaign of Protestant iconoclasm, every last statue and altar was removed, meaning that the interior is exceptionally plain today. The main attraction in the church is the pulpit, adorned with elaborate carvings that took the sculptor Albert Jansz Vinckenbrinck 15 years to complete.

The Nieuwe Kerk has no steeple. Although foundations were laid for one in 1565, political turbulence and religious wars halted construction. By the time things had quietened down, the city council no longer wanted a tower that would have been higher than the dome of the new town hall (today's palace). This certainly speaks to the historic balance of power in Amsterdam. As a compromise, the town hall was pushed back to allow space for at least the high transept of the church to border the square.

Today, the church is used as an exhibition space and has hosted a variety of shows with subjects ranging from Islamic art to Marilyn Monroe. The Nieuwe Kerk is still used for the coronations of Dutch kings and queens, including for King Willem-Alexander in 2013. *Daily 10am–5pm* | *admission varies by exhibit* | *Dam* | *nieuwekerk. nl* | *tram 2, 4,11, 12, 13, 14, 17, 24 Dam* | 🗺 *F3*

🔢 AMSTERDAM DUNGEON

For fans of the ghoulish: an exhibition to send a shiver down your spine. Explore the dark side of Amsterdam's history, including a live show and a ghost train. Cheap ticket deals with Madame Tussaud's. *Sun–Thu 11am–6pm, Fri/Sat till 7pm* | *admission 24 euros* | *Rokin 78* | *the-dungeons.nl* | *metro 52, tram 4, 14, 24 Rokin* | ⏱ *2 hrs* | 🗺 *F4*

SIGHTSEEING

The Koninklijk Paleis had bureaucratic beginnings: it started out as the city hall

🇮🇹 AMSTERDAM MUSEUM

Amid the throngs of shoppers on Kalverstraat, a Baroque gate marks the entrance to the City Museum. Head in and discover the surprisingly large courtyard of this 17th-century former orphanage. An excellent interactive exhibition on the history of the city is inside. After an hour at the museum, you'll come to understand how entrepreneurialism, freedom of thought, civic consciousness and creativity have shaped the city for centuries. *Daily 10am–5pm | admission 13.50 euros (MK) | Kalverstraat 92 | amsterdammuseum.nl | metro 52, tram 4, 14, 24 Rokin or tram 2, 11, 12 Spui | ⏱ 2 hrs | 🗺 F4*

🇮🇹 BEGIJNHOF ★

An oasis of peace and quiet in the buzzing city centre – at least if you come on a weekday and a busload of tourists hasn't just arrived. White houses with lovingly tended, tiny front gardens are grouped around a small church and a few chestnut trees. When it was founded in 1346, the Begijnhof was located on the edge of town. It was a place of residence for single women who wished to live in a religious community but not become nuns. They mainly devoted themselves to caring for elderly people. Two fires almost completely destroyed the Begijnhof in the 15th century and the buildings here today largely date from

37

the 17th century. The house at number 34, by contrast, was built around 1470 and is thought to be the oldest wooden house in the Netherlands. Opposite the English Presbyterian

INSIDER TIP
I spy ... a church?

chapel, a 17th-century Catholic *secret church* is hidden within two residential buildings.

About 100 people still live in the Begijnhof – but the last beguine died in 1971. *Daily 9am–5pm | entrances on Spui and Kalverstraat | metro 52, tram 4, 14, 24 Rokin or tram 2, 11, 12 Spui | ⏱ 30 mins | 🗺 F4*

🄀 SPUI

Spui is regarded as the city's most traditional square. It is surrounded by old Amsterdam pubs such as Café *Luxembourg*, *Zwart* and *Café Hoppe*. The

INSIDER TIP
Traditional tipples

last of these opened in 1670 and retains its dark wood-panelled interior and sandy floor. On Fridays there is a second-hand book market on the square. *Tram 2, 11, 12 Spui | 🗺 F4*

🄀 MUNTTOREN

In the hustle and bustle at the junction of Kalverstraat, Singel and Reguliersbreestraat, it is easy to overlook the "Mint Tower", which dates to 1620, despite the fact that it once played a very important role in the city's defences. When the city of Dordrecht, which had the right to mint coins, was in danger of being occupied by French forces in 1672, gold

Still life *beguine*-style: during the week, the Begijnhof has a villagey feel

and silver coins were minted here for just a few months. *Muntplein 1 | metro 52, tram 4, 14, 24 Rokin | ☐ G4*

GRACHTEN-RING & JORDAAN

The completely preserved historic ★ Grachtenring (Canal Ring) is Amsterdam's biggest attraction – quite literally.

The old canals, Singel, Herengracht, Keizersgracht and Prinsengracht, as well as countless smaller canals that cross these, form a semicircle around the medieval city centre.

In the early 17th century, global trade had made Amsterdam very rich. The beginning of the Golden Age was accompanied by a population boom. Within just 50 years, the number of residents increased fourfold. The old city became too crowded and construction began on the Canal Ring, one of the world's most spectacular urban building projects at the time. Its innovative features were not only the spacious layout of the canals, but also the fact that trees were planted on the banks. Rich merchants built their new residences and warehouses on these waterways, and building plots on the canals were expensive. As the purchase price and later taxation were based on the width of the plot, most houses were built with a narrow front, but then extended to the back. By

1680, the plan to enlarge the city had been completed, and the Canal Ring was encircled by a defensive moat on the site of what is today Stadhouderskade. To this day, living on the Canal Ring is a mark of economic success in Amsterdam.

★ Jordaan – once a district for poor artisans and servants – was built at about the same time as the Canal Ring. It is less upmarket but no less picturesque, and today it is home to many intellectuals and artists. Their galleries and studios ☛ lend the whole area a distinctly villagey feel.

🟤 NOORDERKERK

Although it is hard to believe, the Noorderkerk stood in the middle of a new housing area when it was first built. Today it sits on Noordermarkt, one of Amsterdam's leafiest and most olde-worlde squares. Behind it, houses nestle up close to the church. Completed in 1623, the church is typically Protestant in that the pulpit is the focal point of its layout. *Mon 10.30am–12.30pm, Sat 11am–1pm | Noordermarkt 44 | 10 min walk from the main station | ☐ F2*

🟤 ANNE FRANK HUIS ★

"Dear Kitty …": readers all over the world will recognise the words at the start of entries in Anne Frank's diary. She lived in hiding for two years during World War II with her family in this house on Prinsengracht – only to be deported at the last minute to Bergen-Belsen where she was murdered. Today the house is home to the Anne Frank Foundation and its museum.

A secret door leads to the house at the back and the little flat in which the family was forced to live. Because of the museum's popularity, you can only tour the house if you have booked online well in advance. *April-Oct, daily 9am–10pm; Nov–March, Sun-Fri 9am–7pm & Sat until 9pm; closed on Yom Kippur | admission 10 euros | Prinsengracht 263 | annefrank. org | tram 13, 17 Westermarkt | ⏱ 2 hrs | ⬚ F3*

🔲 WESTERKERK

When it was completed in 1631, the Westerkerk – designed by Hendrick de Keyser – was the world's largest Protestant church. Inside, it is white and bright with restrained ornamentation in the Renaissance style.

However, the ★ *Westertoren*, the 85-m tower affectionately known as "Oude Wester" among Amsterdammers, is more famous than the church itself. It is the emblem of Jordaan and the subject of many songs. Its imperial crown dome houses a glockenspiel with 49 bells. As it is the city's tallest tower, the superb view from the top makes the climb worthwhile. *Church opening hours Mon-Fri, (May-Oct also Sat) 10am–3pm, Glockenspiel Tue 12–1pm, Tower opening hours April-June Mon-Fri 10am–6pm, Sat 10am–8pm, July-Sept Mon-Sat 10am–8pm, Oct Mon-Fri 11am–5pm, Sat 10am–6pm | admission 8 euros | Prinsengracht 281/Westermarkt | tram 13, 17 Westermarkt | ⬚ F3*

Sightseeing on the Canal Ring – best done by boat

🔲 HOMOMONUMENT

Three rust-red marble slabs on the square in front of the Westerkerk are the world's first memorial to persecution against homosexuality. It was installed in 1987, first and foremost in memory of those LGBTQ people who suffered during the Nazi persecution, but today it stands against discrimination everywhere. *Tram 13, 17 Westermarkt | ⬚ F3*

🔲 HOUSEBOAT MUSEUM 👪

On board the old freighter *Hendrika Maria*, you can see with your own eyes what life on a houseboat is like. How do you heat them? What do you with

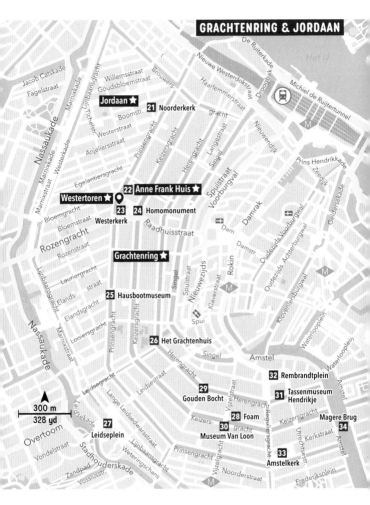

GRACHTENRING & JORDAAN

sewage? Is it very dark under the deck? *Tue–Sun, 10am–5pm | admission 4.50 euros | Prinsengracht 296 K | houseboatmuseum.nl | tram 5, 7, 19 Elandsgracht | ◷ 30 mins | ▥ E–F4*

26 GRACHTENHUIS

In this merchant's house built by Philip Vingboons in 1663, you can learn about the intricacies involved in constructing the Canal Ring, complete with historic maps, miniature canal houses, and a model of the city. *Tue–Sun 10am–5pm | admission 15 euros (MK) | Herengracht 386 | hetgrachtenhuis.nl | tram 2, 11, 12 Koningsplein | ◷ 1 hr | ▥ F4*

27 LEIDSEPLEIN

If you are looking for buzz, this is the place. Tram bells ring, tourists pack the pubs, neon signs flash and street artists perform in this square at the heart of the city. Cinemas, theatres, cafés and restaurants circle Leidseplein, which has thriving night-life, especially at weekends. Head to the balcony of the Stadsschouwburg for the best view of it all. *Tram 1, 2, 7, 11, 12, 19 Leidseplein | ⌑ E5*

INSIDER TIP
The best view of the action

28 FOAM

Fans of contemporary photography should not miss this gallery housed in a 19th-century house on the canal. Its changing exhibitions cover many different aspects of photography, and the café in the basement is a great place for a quiche or slice of cake afterwards. *Sat–Wed 10am–6pm, Thu–Fri 10am–9pm | admission 10 euros (MK) | Keizersgracht 609 | foam. nl | tram 16, 24 Keizersgracht | ⌑ G5*

29 GOUDEN BOCHT ⚑

The "golden arc" of the Herengracht stretches between Leidsestraat and Vijzelstraat. As the name suggests, these houses are noticeably larger and grander than most of the other buildings on the canals. They were built comparably late in the 17th century, when many merchants had already become wealthy bankers who could afford double plots. By then, symmetric neoclassical houses with columned doorways were in fashion. Decorated like real palaces inside, they often have elaborate marble panelling and stucco detail. Has your curiosity been piqued? Unfortunately you're not allowed into number 502, the mayor's residence, but you are more than welcome – indeed encouraged – to pop into Number 672, which is home to the *Museum Van Loon (see next entry). Metro 52 Vijzelstraat, tram 24 Prinsengracht | ⌑ F–G 4–5*

30 MUSEUM VAN LOON

What was life like for the city's upper crust in the 17th and 18th centuries? The answer awaits in this magnificent building. Built in 1671 for a wealthy merchant, the house was owned for a time by Rembrandt's pupil Ferdinand

Museum van Loon: how the other half lived in the 17th century

Bol, and was bought by the wealthy Van Loon family in 1884. The reception rooms, dining rooms and bedrooms are open to visitors. The Baroque canal garden and coach house, which are visible from the small salon, are relics of bygone days. *Daily 10am–5pm | admission 10 euros (MK) | Keizersgracht 672 | metro 52, tram 24 Vijzelstraat | ⏱ 30 mins | 🗺 G5*

🟥31 TASSENMUSEUM HENDRIKJE

From clutches to canvas bags, there are handbags galore on display at the Tassenmuseum, which documents the history of this fashion accessory from the 15th century to the present. Alongside its 4,000-piece collection and a pretty café, the museum's all-too-tempting shop sells designer handbags. *Daily 10am–5pm | admission 12.50 euros | Herengracht 573 | tassenmuseum.nl | tram 4, 14 Rembrandtplein | ⏱ 1 hr | 🗺 G5*

🟥32 REMBRANDTPLEIN

In the 1920s, Rembrandtplein was the hub of the city's art scene. Nowadays this square attracts tourists and night owls because there is always something going on around the Rembrandt statue and the life-size sculptures depicting The Night Watch. For a taste of the 1920s, make a stop at the charming *Café Schiller* at number 24a – don't mix it up with Brasserie Schiller next door! *Tram 4, 14 Rembrandtplein | 🗺 G4–5*

INSIDER TIP
Travel back to the 20s

Magere Brug illuminations

🟥33 AMSTELKERK

The Amstelkerk was built in 1669 because there weren't enough churches on the new Canal Ring. It was only meant to be temporary so they used wood, with the intention of rebuilding in stone later. But this never happened, so this plain white steeple-less church, reminiscent of a cowshed, still stands on Amstelveld. The open space in front of the church with its old trees, playground and outdoor café is one of the nicest spots in Amsterdam. It is also home to a 🐷 good value flower market on Monday mornings. *Amstelveld 10 | tram 4 Prinsengracht | 🗺 G5*

34 MAGERE BRUG 🏴

The Magere Brug looks like it belongs in a Van Gogh painting. Amsterdam's most famous bridge is particularly lovely at night when its lights twinkle like stars. *Kerkstraat | tram 4 Prinsengracht | metro 51, 53, 54 Waterlooplein | ▥ G5*

WATERLOO-PLEIN & PLANTAGE

The area around the *Waterlooplein* was once the Jewish quarter but much of its population was deported and murdered during World War II. Almost the only thing that remains today is the word "Mokum", the Yiddish word for home, which is still one of Amsterdam's nicknames.

Thanks to the Netherlands' tolerance, many Jews resettled in the country from the 17th century. Amsterdam's Jewish quarter was soon populated by both Ashkenazi (German descent) and Sephardic (Portuguese descent) Jews. During World War II, the Nazis brought an abrupt end to the city's flourishing Jewish community. Only 6,000 of Amsterdam's Jews survived the Holocaust. What remains today are several synagogues that are now home to the Jewish Museum, as well as some diamond-cutting shops.

Adjoining to the east is the posh, leafy residential district of *De Plantage*.

The city's former naval arsenal is now the maritime Scheepvaartmuseum

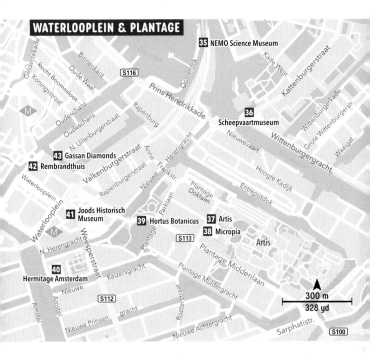

WATERLOOPLEIN & PLANTAGE

35 NEMO Science Museum
S116
Binnenkant
Oude Waal
Recht Boomssloot
Koningsstraat
Gelder.sekade
Prins Hendrikkade
Oosterdok
Kade West
Kattenburgerstraat
Witttenburgerkade
Grote Wittenburgerstraat
Waalgat
36 Scheepvaartmuseum
Nieuwevaart
Wittenburgergracht
Rapenburg
Oudeschans
Oudeschans
N. Uilenburgerstraat
Anne Frankstr.
Nieuwe Herengracht
Hoogte Kadijk
Entrepotdok
43 Gassan Diamonds
42 Rembrandthuis
Valkenburgerstraat
Rapenburgerstraat
Nieuwe Frankstr.
Waterlooplein
Plantage Doklaan
41 Joods Historisch Museum
39 Hortus Botanicus
37 Artis
38 Micropia
S113
Artis
Plantage Parklaan
N. Herengracht
Weesperstraat
Plantage Middenlaan
Artis
40 Hermitage Amsterdam
Keizersgracht
Plantage Muidergracht
Roeterstraat
Nieuwe
S112
Amstel
Nieuwe Prinsen...gracht
Nieuwe Achtergracht
Sarphatistr.
S100

300 m
328 yd

When the Canal Ring was laid out in the 17th century, it did not extend east beyond the Amstel – instead, this area had gardens and shipyards. It was not until the 19th century that the area was redeveloped as a middle-class neighbourhood, and the Entrepotdok customs warehouse was built. Today, visitors come to this green district mainly for the zoo or the botanical garden.

35 NEMO ☻

Star architect Renzo Piano's whale-like NEMO building sits above the entrance to the IJ tunnel. It contains a child-friendly interactive science museum whose best exhibit is the chain reaction which is set off several times a day. *Tue–Sun 10am–5.30pm | admission (4 years plus) 17.50 euros (MK) | Oosterdok 2 | nemoscience museum.nl | 10 mins walk from the Central Station | ⟳ 2 hrs | 🕮 J4*

36 SCHEEPVAARTMUSEUM ☻

This maritime museum, housed in an old naval arsenal dating from the 17th century, has thousands of model ships, old navigation instruments, weapons, charts and paintings that illustrate the glorious history of Dutch seafaring. It also has three interactive exhibitions on whaling, the Golden Age, and the port of Amsterdam today that are particularly geared towards children. The replica of the East Indies ship *Amsterdam* allows visitors to see

Ship Ahoy! close-up what life was like for an 18th century sailor. The original *Amsterdam* didn't sail all seven seas because it sank in a storm off the English coast on its maiden voyage. *Daily 9am–5pm | admission 16 euros (MK) | Kattenburgerplein 1 | scheepvaartmuseum.nl | bus 22, 48 Kadijksplein | ⏱ 2 hrs | ⬚ J4*

37 ARTIS

Amsterdam's Zoo is not very big but it has been excellently put together. The main highlights are the butterfly house, the seal-feeding shows and the old aquarium, where one tank recreates the habitat of an Amsterdam canal – worn-out bikes, cars and plastic waste included. There is also a lemur island where energetic sifakas charge around as though in the wild. *Nov–Feb 9am–5pm, March–Oct 9am–6pm | admission 24 euros, children 3–9 years 20.50 euros | Plantage Kerklaan 38–40 | artis.nl | tram 14 Artis | ⏱ 3 hrs | ⬚ H4*

Underwater Amsterdam

38 MICROPIA

"Urgh! Who wants to go a museum about microbes?" But once you get up close to these mini life forms, you realise just how beautiful they can be. Fungi, algae, bacteria and viruses form the subject of this excellent museum which is particularly well suited for kids over eight. *Sun–Wed 9am–6pm, Thu–Sat 9am–8pm | admission 15 euros, children up to 9 years 13 euros, ticket packages with the zoo | Plantage Kerklaan 38–40 | micropia.nl | tram 14 Artis | ⏱ 1 hr | ⬚ H4*

39 HORTUS BOTANICUS

As one of the oldest botanical gardens in the world, the Hortus combines a bit of botany with a touch of time travel. Over 300 years ago, Dutch doctors began planting this garden full of exotic herbs which merchants and mariners had brought back from their voyages. This soon gave them a head start over their European colleagues in tropical medicine. The old palm house is especially attractive but don't miss the futuristic greenhouse. In the *Hortuswinkel*, you can buy flower bulbs and young plants of rare varieties. *Daily 10am–5pm |*

admission 9.50 euros | Plantage Middenlaan 2 | dehortus.nl | tram 14 Mr. Visserplein | ⏱ 1 hr | 🗺 H4

⁴⁰ HERMITAGE AMSTERDAM

The famous Hermitage art museum in St Petersburg is full to bursting, so some of its collection has been transferred to satellite museums in London, Las Vegas and now Amsterdam. Changing exhibits featuring pieces from the main collection are on display in this former 17th century old people's home. Don't miss the old church hall, the Regency room and especially the fully equipped historic kitchen, where the pensioners' meals were once prepared. *Daily 9am-5pm | admission varies by*

exhibition | Nieuwe Herengracht 14 | hermitage.nl | metro 51, 53, 54 Waterlooplein | ⏱ 2 hrs | 🗺 G5

⁴¹ JOODS HISTORISCH MUSEUM

No fewer than four synagogues from the 17th and 18th centuries form today's Jewish Historical Museum, which lies at the heart of what was once the Jewish quarter. The museum tells the story of the Dutch Jewish community, including the history of their persecution. The temporary exhibitions are usually more light-hearted, with topics ranging from Jewish photography to Amy Winehouse. The museum also has a 🎭 *children's museum* that is furnished like a Jewish family home.

The Hermitage Amsterdam houses surplus art treasures from St Petersburg

Your ticket is also valid in the Portuguese Synagogue next door (which is still used for worship today), in the National Holocaust Museum and in the former Hollandsche Schouwburg, where Jews were brought before being deported. Once a month there are atmospheric candlelit concerts in the Portuguese Synagogue. *Daily 11am–5pm | admission 15 euros (MK) | Jonas Daniël Meijerplein 2-4 | jhm.nl | tram 14 Mr. Visserplein, metro 51, 53, 54 Waterlooplein | ⏱ 2 hrs | 🗺 H4*

> **INSIDER TIP**
> **Classical music by candlelight**

42 REMBRANDTHUIS

Rembrandt van Rijn (1606–1669), the painter of *The Night Watch*, is one of the most famous Amsterdammers of all time. An artistic genius, a troublemaker and a ladies' man, he was born in Leiden, but spent most of his life in Amsterdam. Both his finances and his love life were subject to huge changes in fortune. He bought this house in what was then the Jewish quarter in 1639. Money problems forced him to sell it in 1660 and move into a rented flat before dying as a pauper in 1669. His former house was converted into a museum in 1908. A modern annexe houses the world's largest collection of his etchings, copperplate engravings and drawings. The old part of the house has been furnished as it might have looked in Rembrandt's time, including his studio. *Daily 10am–6pm | admission 13 euros (MK) | Jodenbreestraat 4-6 | rembrandthuis.nl | tram 14 Mr. Visserplein | metro 51, 53, 54 Waterlooplein | ⏱ 1 hr | 🗺 G4*

Financial problems forced Rembrandt to sell his house

43 GASSAN DIAMONDS

Amsterdam was once an international centre of the diamond trade. After World War II this sector declined, but there are still a few cutting workshops left. Many of those that offer tours are purely visitor attractions as the genuine workshops are not usually open to the public. Gassan Diamonds is the exception. In an imposing brick building dating from the late 19th century, 500 employees are engaged in polishing and selling these precious stones. On the 🍴 free tours, visitors follow a stone's journey from a raw diamond to a polished gem. Naturally, this is followed by a sales pitch. *Daily*

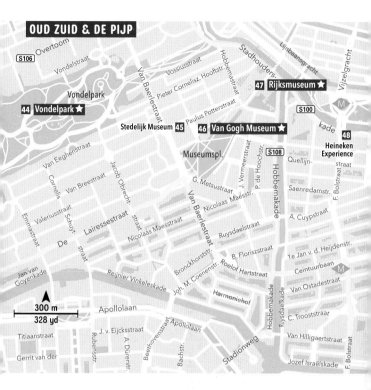

OUD ZUID & DE PIJP

9am–5pm | free admission | Nieuwe Uilenburgerstraat 173–175 | gassan.com | metro 51, 53, 54 Waterlooplein | ⏱ 30 mins | 🗺 H4

OUD ZUID & DE PIJP

To the south-west of Museumplein lies the upmarket district of Oud Zuid. Built in the 19th century, everything in this neighbourhood is a bit plusher than in the rest of the city.

Vondelpark, Amsterdam's "green lung", lies on the north-western edge of this district. Wealthy residents donated the funds for this park so that from their windows they could look out over trees. Today Oud Zuid (the "Old South") remains one of Amsterdam's most exclusive districts, with property prices here only beaten by those on the Canal Ring. It is home to exclusive designer shops, expensive restaurants and the city's best museums. To the east is *De Pijp*, which was built as a working-class quarter around the same time. Thanks to gentrification and urban renewal, the flats in the former tenement buildings are now quite popular with hipsters and young families. As one of the most multicultural districts in the city, *De Pijp* offers a vibrant array of trendy spots to eat, shop or head out on the town at night.

44 VONDELPARK ★

Don't come here looking for a peaceful oasis. On a sunny afternoon you can hardly see the park for all the people in it. Vondelpark is less a green space than a meeting place, bicycle route, event venue and playground for Amsterdammers. Back in the 1960s, it was a magnet for hippies from all over the world, who set up camp until the police put an end to the squatting in 1975. But its origins were much more conventional. The 120-acre space, named after the Renaissance poet Joost van den Vondel, was the first public park in Amsterdam when it was created in 1865. Well-off citizens got together to create an oasis of greenery in front of their new villas to the south of the Canal Ring. Vondelpark is home to a *stage* where ☛ *free open-air*

PARK TAKE-OVER

When you walk through Vondelpark in summer, you hear them squawking; in winter, when the branches of the trees are bare, you can see them: bright green parakeets. To be precise, they are ring-necked parakeets, a type of Asian parrot that is commonly kept as a pet in Europe. In 1976 an owner released his mating pair in Vondelpark because they made too much noise. It didn't take long for the birds to breed, and park's trees provide comfortable places to roost. At sundown hundreds of parakeets gather there every day and stage a deafening, cacophonous concert. The local residents are none too keen on them, and neither are the Dutch animal protection authorities, as these invaders compete with native birds for places to breed and supplies of food.

A victory for modern art: Dan Flavin's installation in the Stedelijk Museum

performances are held in summer (openluchttheater.nl, ▢ D6) – with everything from children's theatre to salsa on the menu. One of Amsterdam's few beer gardens, the *Blauwe Theehuis*, sits directly behind it. *Tram 1, 11 Eerste Constantijn Huygensstraat, 3 Van Baerlestraat, 2 Cornelis Schuytstraat | ▢ C–E 5–6*

45 STEDELIJK MUSEUM

The Stedelijk Museum holds one of the most significant collections of contemporary art in the Netherlands. A futuristic bathtub-shaped annexe was added to the 19th century main building in 2012. In it, work by artists from Monet and Mondrian to Malevich and Bruce Naumann are exhibited in an unconventional space designed by Rem Koolhaas. The original building and its bright rooms are now only used for temporary exhibitions of modern art. *Daily 10am–6pm, Fri until 10pm | admission 18.50 euros (MK) | Paulus Potterstraat 13 | stedelijk. nl | tram 2, 5, 12 Van Baerlestraat, 3 Museumplein | ⏱ 2 hrs | ▢ E6*

Rembrandt's *The Night Watch* pulls in the crowds to the Rijksmuseum

46 VAN GOGH MUSEUM ★

Just about everyone in the world knows *Sunflowers*, *The Bedroom* and *The Potato Eaters*. Van Gogh remains one of the most expensive and most popular artists of all time. The state-run Van Gogh Museum owns the world's largest collection of works by the great man. This was made possible by the otherwise regrettable fact that almost none of Vincent van Gogh's (1853–1890) paintings found a buyer in his lifetime. He gifted them to his brother as a token of gratitude for the latter's financial support. As a result, the paintings stayed in the family, who then bequeathed 205 paintings and 500 drawings to the museum in 1963. The exhibition traces the tragic life of the artist from his early years in the Netherlands to his time in Paris and the south of France, and his death in Auvers-sur-Oise.

In 1999, a new three-storey annexe was constructed next to the older part of the museum, designed by Gerrit Rietveld. An underground passage connects the two buildings and houses the entrance to the museum. You must book online for a specific time slot before you arrive. *Daily 9am–6pm, Fri until 9pm | admission 18 euros (MK) | Museumplein 6 | vangoghmuseum.nl | tram 2, 5, 12 Van Baerlestraat, 3 Museumplein | ⏱ 2 hrs | 🗺 E6*

47 RIJKSMUSEUM ★

Designed by the architect Pierre Cuypers, who is also responsible for the main station, the museum opened to the public in 1885. Thanks to its ornate style, it looks more like a castle or cathedral than a museum at first glance. This actually caused a bit of a stir when the building first opened because the Protestant king, Willem III, refused to step foot in "this archbishop's palace". But this doesn't seem to bother any of the two million annual visitors to the museum.

The entrance is located in a bicycle and pedestrian tunnel under the building. Once you leave the modern foyer, the elaborately decorated walls of the historic exhibition rooms serve as the backdrop for a veritable treasure trove of artworks with a focus on the Dutch Golden Age. It almost seems as if the museum was built around Rembrandt's famous painting *The Night Watch*, which sits in glory at the end of the gallery of honour. The men who commissioned the painting in 1642 were not pleased with Rembrandt's work because they felt that the members of Captain Frans Banning Cocq's shooting company had not been portrayed in an honourable enough manner. But this is precisely what makes the painting a masterpiece. It is incredibly dynamic and more realistic than the other military portraits of the day.

The other galleries exhibit the works of other Dutch painters such as Frans Hals, Jan Steen, Jacob van Ruisdael and Jan Vermeer. There is always a crowd in front of Vermeer's *The Milk Maid* (1660) and *Woman in Blue Reading a Letter* (1662-64). Genre scenes such as these give a striking impression of life in Dutch merchants' households in the 17th century – as does Jan Steen's *La Toilette* (1663), which depicts a young woman dressing in the morning. Don't miss the beautiful historic library that can be seen from gallery 1.13. In the stairwell of the Philips wing, modern design meets history with the *Shylight* sculpture by Studio Drift which creates a poetic ballet of light and shadows. *Daily 9am-5pm | admission 17.50 euros (MK), free for under-18s | Stadhouderskade 42 | rijksmuseum.nl | metro 52 Vijzelgracht, tram 2, 5, 12 Rijksmuseum | ⏱ 3 hrs | ▥ F5*

INSIDER TIP
Let light dance

48 HEINEKEN EXPERIENCE

Beer is no longer produced in the old Heineken brewery on Stadhouderskade, and the building has been converted into a visitor attraction where you can learn about Heineken's history. Two "free" *biertjes* finish the tour. *Mon-Thu 11am-5.30pm, Fri-Sun 10.30am-7pm | admission 21 euros | Stadhouderskade 78 | metro 52 Vijzelgracht, tram 24 Marie Heinekenplein | ⏱ 1-1½ hrs | ▥ F6*

OTHER SIGHTS

49 A'DAM ★

The erstwhile Shell office tower on the north shore of the IJ stood empty for a long time before the city sold it to a trio of investors from the clubbing scene in 2015. They have turned it into a house that never sleeps. The club *Shelter* is located in the basement, while the burger restaurant *The*

Butcher Social Club occupies the ground floor. The upper floors are home to the *Sir Adam Hotel* as well as offices for music companies. In the round "neck" of the high-rise building, you'll find fine dining in the revolving *Moon* restaurant, just under the *Madam* cocktail bar.

But the biggest attraction is by far the *lookout platform (daily 10.30am–9pm | admission 14.50 euros, swing 5 euros extra)* on the roof which offers an incredible view of the city. For a real rush, let your legs dangle over the side of the building on Europe's highest swing. *Overhoeksplein 1 | adamtoren.nl | free ferry to Buiksloterweg from the northern side of the main station | ⌁ G2*

🔟 THIS IS HOLLAND

If you have wondered what the complex irrigation and water defence systems which make up the Dutch landscape look like to birds … this 5-D film is the thing for you. As you fly around, the wind blows through your hair and your seat moves. *Daily 10am–8pm | admission 16.50 euros | Overhoeksplein 51 | thisisholland.com | free ferry to Buiksloterweg from the northern side of the main station | ⏱ 45 mins (flight experience 10 mins) | ⌁ G2*

🔟 EYE FILM INSTITUTE 🍸

It would be hard not to notice the futuristic white architecture of the Eye Film Institute, which sits on the northern bank of the IJ next to the A'DAM

Keep an eye out for the Eye Film Institute: a cinephile's paradise

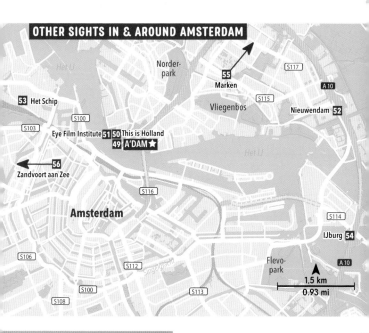

OTHER SIGHTS IN & AROUND AMSTERDAM

Norderpark

55 Marken

S117

A 10

53 Het Schip

S115

Vliegenbos

Nieuwendam **52**

S100

S103

Eye Film Institute **51 50** This is Holland
49 A'DAM ★

Het IJ

56
Zandvoort aan Zee

S116

Amsterdam

S114

IJburg **54**

S106

S112

Flevopark

A 10

1.5 km
0.93 mi

S100

S113

S108

tower. It was designed by the Austrian architects Delugan Meissl. Behind its sculptural façade lies the Dutch Film Museum with four cinema screens, 1,200 square metres of exhibition space, a museum shop and a waterfront café. The shop has all the usual souvenirs alongside a good collection of memorabilia.

INSIDER TIP
Souvenirs for film buffs

Exhibition daily 10am–7pm | admission 10.50 euros | Café daily 10am–1am | IJpromenade 1 | eyefilm.nl | free ferry to Buiksloterweg from the north side of the main station | ⊞ G2

52 NIEUWENDAM

If you want to get away from the noise and crowds of the city and see Dutch village life without taking a long journey, look no further than Nieuwendammerdijk. Quaint old houses line the bank, and the small café on the harbour is gloriously traditional. *Metro 52 Noorderpark, then 8 mins walk to the north on Adelaarsweg, Bus 291 Merelstraat | ⅏ M–N1*

53 HET SCHIP

This social housing block, shaped like a ship with its curves and other rounded features, was designed by Michel de Klerk in 1919 and is a great example of Brick Expressionism. A small (functionless) tower graces one side, while the façade on the other has cigar-shaped curves. It is also home to a *post office* and a *historic flat* with original furnishings as well as a museum that tells the story of this rather unique architectural school. *Tue–Sun 11am–5pm | admission 15 euros (MK) | Oostzaanstraat 45 | bus 22, 48 Spaarndammerstraat | ⏱ 1 hr | ⅏ E1*

54 IJBURG

To the east of Amsterdam, a new archipelago is arising in the IJsselmeer. Seven artificial islands are being created to form the new district of IJburg, with space for 45,000 people to live and work. Fans of modern architecture will find plenty to interest them here. For example, on the Brigantijnkade, colourful floating houses bob on jetties. In contrast to houseboats, they have the dimensions and amenities of a normal house, plus you can park your boat outside the front door. Interested? Number 20 is run as a bed and breakfast. *(Ca'Mirandolina | Brigantijnkade 20 | camirandolina.com | tram 26 Steigereiland) | ⅏ 0*

AROUND AMSTERDAM

55 MARKEN

24km / 40 mins on bus 315 from the central station

This village has been isolated from the mainland since the St Julian's Day flood of 1164. Splendid seclusion has helped turn it into a picturesque paradise. Cottages snuggle together by the quayside, sailing boats bob up and down in the harbour, and some older people still wear traditional costume. place tends to attract tourists, especially at the weekend, but most of them stick to the main streets in town. You can easily escape the crowds by making your way through the smaller

side streets or taking a walk along the dyke to the lighthouse. In the evening the place empties out so it is well worth spending the night – try *Hof van Marken (Buurt II 15 | tel. 0299 60 13 00 | hofvanmarken.nl)* – also a popular spot for locals to have their evening pint. *Take metro 52 from the central station to Amsterdam Noord. From there the 315 bus goes to Marken every 30 mins (return trip to Marken with the Waterlanddag-Kaart bought from the driver – 10 euros).*

INSIDER TIP
Marken by moonlight

If you feel like cycling there, you can get to Marken within two hours of pleasant riding (approx. 22km). Behind the main station, take the ferry to IJplein, ride along Meeuwenlaan, turn right onto Nieuwendammerdijk, then stay on the dyke by the IJsselmeer. After the village of Uitdam turn right again and on to Marken on the connecting dyke. ⊞ 0

56 ZANDVOORT AAN ZEE

30km / 33 mins by train from the central station

It takes barely half an hour by train to get to Zandvoort aan Zee, the North Sea resort on Amsterdam's doorstep. With its high-rises and faceless apartment blocks, this is not an attractive place but to make up for that there is a long, long sandy beach, and you only need to walk along it a short way to leave the town behind.

On warm summer weekends it can be crowded here, but outside the peak season you will have only the gulls (and some intrepid walkers) for company. Make sure you buy something from the traditional fishing carts that are pulled across the beach by tractors. They sell all sorts of deep-fried food and delicious prawn rolls. *Trains to Zandvoort every 30 mins from the main station, in winter change at Haarlem | return ticket 11.20 euros |* ⊞ 0

Too crowded in the city? Marken is barely an hour away

EATING & DRINKING

Cambodian, Ethiopian, Peruvian or Surinamese – visitors can go on a culinary world tour in Amsterdam's restaurants.

And some connoisseurs would say that is probably a good thing, because Dutch food itself doesn't have a great reputation. Calvinism regarded all culinary pleasure as unnecessary, even sinful, and for centuries the people of Holland preferred to eat what was plain and nourishing. *Stamppot* is a great example: mashed potato mixed with sausage or meat and cabbage.

A local favourite since time immemorial: *poffertjes*. Try them with syrup

Recently, Dutch cuisine has got better. Chefs in good restaurants are reinventing local and seasonal specialities, rediscovering forgotten vegetables and experimenting with influences from all over the globe. Dishes from former Dutch colonies have also firmly embedded themselves in the national food scene. Every child in Amsterdam knows what *nasi goreng* (rice with shrimps and chicken) and *saté* (skewered chicken with peanut sauce) are. The city's Indonesian restaurants are among the best in Europe. And in Chinatown you can try authentic Chinese food.

WHERE AMSTERDAM EATS

PONT 13 ★

First a bite to eat, then a spot of shopping

HAARLEMMERDIJK

JORDAAN

LINDENGRACHT

This market is packed full of culinary classics

WEST

A full range of global cuisines, plus some lovely local restaurants

Moeders ★

DE HALLEN & UMGEBUNG

CENTRUM

FuLu Mandarijn ★

Foodhallen ★

Café Américain ★

WEST

Amsterdam's most diverse neighbourhood – with Surinamese snacks and oyster bars

DE PIJP

OUD-

Blauw ★

ZUID

MARCO POLO HIGHLIGHTS

★ **FOODHALLEN**
There will be something for everyone here ➤ p. 62

★ **CAFÉ AMÉRICAIN**
Grand café in elegant Art Deco style ➤ p. 63

★ **GREETJE**
Pleasure of a rare kind: modern Dutch cuisine, from sea vegetables to black pudding ➤ p. 66

★ **BLAUW**
Authentic Indonesian cooking ➤ p. 67

★ **DE PLANTAGE**
Watch the flamingos while you eat ➤ p. 67

★ **FULU MANDARIJN**
A Chinese restaurant on three floors ➤ p. 68

★ **MOEDERS**
Traditional Dutch fare the way your "moeder" makes it ➤ p. 69

★ **PONT 13**
Excellent bistro food on an old ferry with lots of atmosphere ➤ p. 70

NOORD

Het IJ

Meeuwenla...

Amsterdam's Chinatown
ZEEDIJK

Piet Heinkade

IJhaven

Eitshaven

S116

Piet Hein-Tunnel

HAVENS-

Entrepohaven

OOST

⚲ **Greetje** ★

Kattenburgerstr.

Oostenburgergracht

Panamalaan

Water-looplein

⚲ **De Plantage** ★

Middenlaan

Zeeburgerdijk

Weesperstr.

Mauritskade

Molukken-straat

Flevoweg

JAVASTRAAT

Options from all over the world – from Ghana to Iraq and Vietnam

Insulindeweg

Flevo-park

M Weesperplein

Oosterp...

straat

S112

M Wibautstraat

Wibautstraat

WIBAUTSTRAAT

Linnaeusstraat

S113

OOST

Hip, hipper, hippest

Middenweg

Amsteldijk

S110

500 m
547 yd

There is a restaurant or street-food stand on almost every corner. Prices are relatively high and service can take some getting used to. Standards may not be top notch but staff are generally good humoured and friendly. The traditional *eetcafés*, serving mostly Dutch food with a Mediterranean touch, are good for visitors on a budget.

Be careful: what gets called a café in the Netherlands is often more like a bar or pub and everyone knows that coffee shops sell more than just coffee!

EETCAFÉS

DE BAKKERSWINKEL
In a building that once belonged to the Westergasfabriek gasworks, a branch of the small Bakkerswinkel chain serves delicious sandwiches, muffins and cakes made with regional organic ingredients. *Daily | Polonceaukade 1–2 | tel. 020 6 88 06 32 | tram 5 Van Hallstraat | West | ▥ E1*

MORLANG
Creative international cuisine and youthful vibes in a grand canalside house. The tables upstairs are nicer than in the basement. *Daily | Keizersgracht 451 | tel. 020 6 25 26 81 | tram 2, 11, 12 Keizersgracht | Centrum | ▥ F4*

PIET DE LEEUW
Traditional Amsterdam *eetcafé* that is famous for its steak – adventurous eaters can try horse steaks here. Horse is a common meat in the Netherlands and is said to be very tender. Anyone? *Daily | Noorderstraat 11 | tel. 020 6 23 71 81 | metro 52, tram 24 Vijzelgracht | Centrum | ▥ F5*

INSIDER TIP
Why the long face?

WINKEL 43
This small café has piles of cinnamon-spiced apples wherever you look, which are used in its *famous appeltaart mit slagroom*. It is always packed – especially on Saturdays. *Daily | Noordermarkt 43 | tel. 020 6 23 02 23 | tram 3 Marnixplein | Centrum | f F2*

FOOD COURTS

FOODHALLEN ★
The idea here is that you can eat your way around the whole world in one market hall. Twenty stalls are grouped around a central bar in this old tram depot. From spring rolls to burgers and koftas, there is plenty of choice. *Sun–Thu 11am–11.30pm, Fri/Sat 11am–1am | Bellamyplein 51 | tram 7, 17 Kinkerstraat | West | ▥ D4*

THE FOOD DEPARTMENT
The top floor of the magnificent former post office – now the Magna Plaza shopping centre – is occupied by a food court with 14 stalls. The range includes excellent Chinese food, tacos, seafood and cocktails. *Daily 10am–10pm | Nieuwezijds Voorburgwal 182 | tram 2, 11, 12, 13, 17 Dam | Centrum | ▥ F3*

A warehouse with food from all over the world – Foodhallen

GRAND CAFÉS

CAFÉ AMÉRICAIN ★
Elegant Art Nouveau café in the hotel of the same name. Tiffany lamps, wood panelling and cosy reading chairs bring the 1920s to life. *Daily | Leidseplein 97 | tel. 020 5 56 30 10 | tram 1, 2, 7, 11, 19 Leidseplein | Centrum | □ E5*

DE JAREN
A large café with a restaurant upstairs. In summer, reserve a table on the terrace, where you get a wonderful view of the city. *Daily | Nieuwe Doelenstraat 20–22 | tel. 020 6 25 57 71 | metro 52, tram 4, 14, 24 Rokin | Centrum | □ G4*

GRAND CAFÉ 1E KLAS
Station cafés are not often particularly inviting but this is an exception, serving hamburgers and croquettes in a historic, luxurious fin-de-siècle setting. *Daily | Stationsplein 15 | platform 2b in the main station | tel. 020 6 25 01 31 | metro 51, 52, 53, 54, tram 2, 4, 11, 12, 13, 14, 17, 26 Centraal Station | Centrum | □ G3*

RESTAURANTS €€€

& MOSHIK
Moshik Roth's restaurant is the proud bearer of two Michelin stars They offer small and large "inspiration menus" … at a price. Prepare to spend around 250 euros per person. *Closed Mon/ Tue | Oosterdokskade 5 | tel.*

Organic grub in a greenhouse: De Kas

020 2 60 20 94 | moshikrestaurant. com | 5 min walk from the main station | Centrum | ⚏ H3

BLAUW AAN DE WAL

In the middle of the red-light district, a narrow alley leads to this gastronomic oasis. The courtyard was once part of a monastery. Outstanding French cuisine and good service. Closed Sun | Oudezijds Achterburgwal 99 | tel. 020 3 30 22 57 | metro 51, 53 Nieuwmarkt | Centrum | ⚏ G3

C

C stands for Celsius at renowned chef Michiel van der Eerde's restaurant, in which the cooking temperatures play a big part in the menu. Daily |

Wibautstraat 125 | tel. 020 2 10 30 11 | c.amsterdam | metro 51, 53, 54 Wibautstraat | Oost | ⚏ H6

D'VIJFF VLIEGHEN

Wooden gin barrels, Rembrandt etchings and a collection of old weapons enhance the authenticity of these five 17th-century houses. The menu also upholds Dutch traditions. Daily | Spuistraat 294–302 | tel. 020 5 30 40 60 | metro 52 Rokin, tram 2, 11, 12 Spui | Centrum | ⚏ F4

DE KAS

Organic vegetables from the restaurant's own garden are served in a huge greenhouse. Really modern Dutch food presented in a beautiful setting. Bookings necessary in the evening! Closed Sun | Kamerlingh Onneslaan 3 | tel. 020 4 62 45 62 | tram 19 Hoogweg | Oost | ⚏ K7

DE SILVEREN SPIEGEL

Old-school restaurant in a crooked house dating from 1614. The emphasis is on regional products and contemporary interpretations of Dutch dishes. Closed Sun | Kattengat 4–6 | tel. 020 6 24 65 89 | tram 2, 11, 12, 13, 17 Nieuwezijds Kolk | Centrum | ⚏ G3

ENVY

Hip restaurant with a stylish modern interior design in a long, narrow room, it sits on Prinsengracht. Guests sit together eating small plates at a long counter. You can choose a good vintage from the really extensive wine list. Daily | Prinsengracht 381 | tel.

Today's specials

Snacks

PATAT OORLOG
French fries with mayonnaise, peanut sauce and onions

RUNDVLEESKROKET
Beef croquette

BITTERBALLEN
Deep-fried meatballs with mustard on the side

HOLLANDSE NIEUWE
Pickled herring with gherkins and onions

SAUCIJZENBROODJE
The Dutch take on a sausage roll

Main dishes

MOSSELEN
Mussels cooked in white wine or beer, with chips and mayonnaise

STAMPPOT
Mashed potatoes with salami or meat and vegetables

ROTI
Indian or Surinamese dish consisting of a flat-bread filled with spicy meat or vegetables

KIPSATÉ
Indonesian chicken kebabs with peanut sauce

ERWTENSOEP
A thick pea soup served with brown bread and bacon

Desserts

APPELTAART
Apple tart served with or without whipped cream

POFFERTJES
Mini pancakes served with butter and icing sugar

OLIEBOLLEN
Raisin doughnuts dusted in icing sugar

Drinks

WITBIER
Wheat beer, brewed with citrus fruits and coriander

KOFFIE VERKEERD
A "wrong way round" coffee (with lots of warm milk)

GENEVER
The Dutch precursor to London Gin

020 3 44 64 07 | tram 13, 17 Wester-markt | Centrum | ⏣ E–F4

GREETJE ★

Restaurant with a relaxed atmosphere, hidden away in a side street. Modern Dutch cuisine, from halibut with for-aged coastal vegetables to crème brûlée with liquorice root. If you want to try as many of their crea-tions as possible, order the "grote begin" starter plate. *Closed Mon | Peperstraat 23 | tel. 020 7 79 74 50 | metro 51, 53, 54 Nieuwmarkt | Centrum | ⏣ H4*

INSIDER TIP
A bit of everything

GUTS & GLORY

This small bistro near Rembrandtplein offers a different set menu (4 or 6 courses) each week, which focuses on either particular ingredients or cui-sines. *Daily | Utrechtsestraat 6 | tel. 020 3 62 00 30 | gutsglory.nl | tram 14 Rembrandtplein | Centrum | ⏣ G4*

HOTEL DE GOUDFAZANT

Trendy restaurant in an industrial district in Noord. French-influenced Dutch dishes are served beneath huge chandeliers in a large ware-house. *Closed Mon | Aambeeldstraat 10h | tel. 020 6 36 51 70 | bus 38 Hamerstraat | Noord | ⏣ K2*

VAN VLAANDEREN

Top quality French cuisine with friendly vibes. *Closed Sun/ Mon | Weteringsschans 175 | tel. 020 6 22 82 92 | metro 52, tram 1, 7, 19, 24 Vijzelgracht | Centrum | ⏣ G6*

VUURTORENEILAND

A boat trip and dinner in one. In summer, dinner is served in a green-house on this tiny lighthouse islet. In winter, you eat in the old fort. As they don't have electricity, the entire five-course menu is cooked on an open fire or in a smoker. Online booking essential. The whole experience including the 40-minute crossing takes about five hours and costs 100 euros including drinks. *Departure Wed–Sat 6.30pm, Sun 4pm | Lloyd Hotel quay | Oostelijke Handelskade 34 | tram 26 Rietlandpark | vuurtoren eiland.nl | Oost | ⏣ 0*

YAMAZOTO

This Michelin-starred restaurant in the Japanese Okura Hotel feels very authentic with its own fishpond and the staff wearing traditional Japanese dress. The sashimi is served on ice, the beef raw with a hot griddle. *Daily | Ferdinand Bolstraat 333 | tel. 020 6 88 35 1 | tram 12 Cornelis Troostplein | Zuid | ⏣ F7*

@ SAMBA KITCHEN

A Brazilian all-you-can-eat meat barbe-cue for a fixed price of 27.50 euros (including sides). *Daily | Ceintuurbaan 63 | tel. 020 6 76 05 13 | metro 52 De Pijp, tram 3, 12, 24 Ferdinand Bolstraat | Zuid | ⏣ F7*

ADAM & SIAM

Are you having trouble deciding whether you want to go for Dutch or Thai food? This bistro in an old tobacco

Authentic and award-winning: Yamazoto serves Japanese cuisine of the finest quality

warehouse offers both. The menu features rib-eye steak with roasted pumpkin alongside green beef curry with coconut milk. *Daily | Rokin 93 | tel. 020 7 77 00 80 | metro 52 Rokin, tram 4, 14, 24 | Centrum | ⌖ F4*

BLAUW ⭐

"Rijstafel" – rice with various curries – is a staple of Indonesian restaurants but this is more authentic than most. Excellent veggie options and Indonesia's spiciest sambal. *Daily | Amstelveenseweg 158–160 | tel. 020 6 75 50 00 | tram 2 Amstelveenseweg | West | ⌖ C6*

CAFÉ DE PONT

This charming restaurant is right next to the quay for the IJ ferry. In summer you can sit outside with a nice view across the water. Changing daily menu with small plates at a reasonable price. *Daily | Buiksloterweg 3–5 | tel. 020 6 36 33 88 | free ferry from Hauptbahnhof to Buiksloterwegveer | Noord | ⌖ H2*

DE GOUDEN REAEL

Simple bistro cooking in an attractive 17th-century building. Adults can tuck into mussels, steak and chicken while 🕿 kids can have hot dogs. *Daily | Zandhoek 14 | tel. 020 6 23 38 83 | bus 48 Barentszplein | West | ⌖ F1*

DE PLANTAGE ⭐

Flamingos for dinner! Although thankfully not on your plate. Modern bistro food in the prettiest conservatory in Amsterdam. In the summer you can sit on the patio and watch flamingos and spoonbills bathing. *Daily | Plantage Kerklaan 36 | tel. 020 7 60 86 00 | tram 14 Artis | Centrum | ⌑ H4*

DE ROZENBOOM
This tiny restaurant with its antique Dutch interior has a menu to match its ambience. Choose from pancakes, soups, *stamppot* and other classic Dutch dishes. *Closed Sun | Rozenboomsteeg 6 | tel. 020 6 22 50 24 | metro 52, tram 4, 14, 24 Rokin | Centrum | ⌑ E4*

DE STRUISVOGEL
Decent bistro food in a tiny cellar. Various three-course menus for 25 euros. All the meat is organic. *Daily | Keizersgracht 312 | tel. 020 23 38 17 | tram 13, 17 Westermarkt | Centrum | ⌑ F4*

FULU MANDARIJN ★
This multi-storey restaurant lacks a bit of character but does serve excellent Chinese food. At lunchtime it is full of families tucking into large meals. Lots of specials and more interesting dishes than those you might associate with your average Chinese takeaway. *Daily | Rokin 26 | Tel. 020 6 23 08 85 | fulumandarijn.com | metro 52 Rokin | Centrum | ⌑ F4*

GARTINE
This daytime spot is in a side street off Kalverstraat. The owners serve produce from their own vegetable garden and regional products in dishes ranging from beef salad with roast pumpkin to sausage made from Beemsterland pork. *Wed–Sun 10am–6pm | Taksteeg 7 | tel. 020 3 20 32 | metro 52, tram 14, 24 Rokin | Centrum | ⌑ F4*

HAPPYHAPPYJOYJOY
A brightly coloured pop interior is the perfect backdrop for Asian street food. Eat your way through Thai, Vietnamese, Indonesian and Chinese specialities, alongside a freezing cold beer. *Daily | Oostelijke Handelskade 4 | tel. 020 3 44 64 33 | tram 26 Rietlandpark | Oost | ⌑ K3*

IN STOCK
The concept behind In Stock is to use food that others throw away. So 80 per cent of their ingredients come from supermarket rejects like bendy cucumbers or oranges which fell out of their nets – but everything is in date. There is set three- or four-course menu each day. Who knew rubbish could taste this good! *Daily | Czaar Peterstraat 21 | tel. 020 3 63 57 65 | instock.nl | tram 7 Eerste Coehoornstraat | Oost | ⌑ K4*

JAPANESE PANCAKE WORLD
And you thought pancakes were a Dutch speciality? Think again – they are also a popular fast food in Japan. In this restaurant near the Westermarkt, you can watch the staff conjure up gloriously unhealthy okonomiyake in front of your eyes. *Closed Mon/ Sun | Tweede Egelantiersdwarsstraat 24a | tel. 020 3 20 44 47 | japanese pancakeworld.com | tram 5 Marnixplein | Centrum | ⌑ E3*

Pata Negra offers authentic tapas right in the heart of Amsterdam

L'ENTRECÔTE ET LES DAMES

This bistro is always packed before and after concerts in the nearby Concertgebouw. It won't take you long to decide what to order because there is only one starter, a salad with walnuts, which is followed by either entrecôte or sole with fries. However, when it comes to dessert you can choose between ten tempting French classics. *Daily | No reservations | Van Baerlestraat 47–49 | entrecote-et-les-dames.nl | tram 3, 5, 12 Museumplein | Zuid | ⊞ E6*

LT. CORNELIS

Like the 17th-century portraits hanging on the walls, the food here is traditionally Dutch, but has a decidedly modern twist. *Daily | Voetboogstraat 13 | tel. 020 2 61 48 63 | metro 52, tram 4, 14, 24 Rokin | Centrum | ⊞ F4*

MOEDERS ★

Home food just the way mum cooks it – which is why the walls here are covered with hundreds of photos of mothers. The menu is traditionally Dutch, but there are a few dishes that might have been rustled up by a Mediterranean mama. *Daily | Rozengracht 251 | tel. 020 6 26 79 57 | tram 13, 17 Marnixstraat | Centrum | ⊞ E4*

Bazar is so richly decorated that it can be hard to focus on your food

NEW KING

A low-lit Chinese restaurant that is always packed. Chinese classics, but also some more unusual dishes ranging from aubergine with tofu to stuffed squid. No reservations! *Daily | Zeedijk 115–117 | tel. 020 6 25 21 80 | Metro 51, 53, 54 Nieuwmarkt | Centrum | ⊞ G3*

PATA NEGRA

A whiff of Spain in Amsterdam: walk through the door of this full and noisy tapas restaurant and you'll think you've been beamed to Seville. Hams hang from the ceilings and wine is served in ceramic jugs. *Daily | Utrechtsestraat 124 | tel. 020 4 22 62 50 | tram 4 Prinsengracht | Centrum | ⊞ G5*

PONT 13 ★

This converted IJ ferry, which is now moored in a remote corner of the harbour, has a terrific atmosphere. Excellent food from fish to burgers. *Daily | Haparandadam 50 | tel. 020 7 70 27 22 | pont13.nl | bus 48 Haparandaweg | West | ⊞ 0*

REM EILAND

In the 1960s this slightly odd tower construction, now in the Oude Houthaven, stood in the North Sea and housed a pirate radio transmitter, and later a water measurement station. In 2011 it was relocated to the harbour and converted into a restaurant with a stunning view. The kitchen serves up modern Dutch and Mediterranean cuisine. *Daily |*

Haparandadam 45 | tel. 020 6 88 55 01 | bus 48 Haparandaweg | West | ᗕ 0

RIJSEL
Rijsel is the Flemish name for the northern French city of Lille whose rustic charm infuses this rotisserie restaurant. Simple but perfectly prepared dishes from Breton fish soup to côte de boeuf with roast potatoes. *Closed Sun | Marcusstraat 52b | tel. 020 4 63 21 42 | rijsel.com | metro 51, 53, 54 Wibautstraat | Oost | ᗕ H7*

THE AVOCADO SHOW
Avocados have become the hippest veg of them all. Hip enough that this restaurant serves nothing else. You can have them on toast or with pancakes and eggs. There is even a cheesecake. *Daily 9am–5pm | No reservations | Daniel Stalpertstraat 61 | metro 52 De Pijp, tram 24 Marie Heinekenplein | Zuid | ᗕ F6*

WORST
Homemade sausages and wine steal the show at this bar. The guests sit on stools around large tables and can watch the chefs cooking away in the open kitchen. *Daily | Barentszstraat 171 | tel. 020 6 25 61 67 | deworst. nl | tram 3 Zoutkeetsgracht | Centrum | ᗕ F1*

RESTAURANTS €

@ WARUNG MARLON
Surinamese place on Albert Cuyp-markt serving up popular *saoto* soup (chicken broth with lemongrass and egg) and fried bananas. *Daily | No reservations | Eerste Van der Helststraat 55 | metro 52 De Pijp | Zuid | ᗕ F6*

BAZAR
Lively Middle Eastern restaurant on Albert Cuypmarkt, with gloriously kitsch décor. Delicious breakfast from 11am. *Daily | Albert Cuypstraat 182 | tel. 020 6 75 05 44 | metro 52 De Pijp, tram 24 Marie Heinekenplein | Zuid | ᗕ G6*

BIRD
Pictures of Thailand's king and queen adorn the walls while the sound system blares Asian pop music. A fun, colourful and loud takeaway. Don't confuse it with the more expensive restaurant of the same name across the way! *Daily | Zeedijk 77 | tel. 020 4 20 62 89 | metro 51, 53, 54 Nieuwmarkt | Centrum | ᗕ G3*

BURGERMEESTER
This small restaurant chain offers juicy burgers of all kinds, served just as you like it: rare, medium or well done. No reservations! *Daily | Utrechtsestraat 8 | tram 4, 14 Rembrandtplein | Centrum | ᗕ F4*

FOU FOW RAMEN
Large bowls filled with steaming hot Japanese noodle soup, with veggie options and treats for spice fans. Throw in some gyoza dumplings too. A great mid-shopping energy boost. *Closed Mon | Elandsgracht 2a | tram 5, 13, 17, 19 Elandsgracht | Centrum | ᗕ E4*

KADIJK

This place looks like an ordinary café on the outside, but they serve excellent Indonesian food. Delicious mackerel. *Daily | Kadijksplein 5 | tel. 020 1 77 44 41 | bus 22 Kadijkslpein | Centrum | ☲ H4*

PALOMA BLANCA

Sweet peppermint tea and delicious couscous are on offer at this Moroccan restaurant. No alcohol. *Closed Mon | Jan Pieter Heijestraat 145 | tel. 020 7 71 46 06 | tram 7, 17 Jan Pieter Heijestraat | West | ☲ D5*

PANCAKES!

A tiny, child-friendly pancake restaurant on a busy shopping street. Deliciously thin pancakes. No reservations! *Daily | Berenstraat 38 | tram 13, 17 Westermarkt | Centrum | ☲ F4*

PANNENKOEKENBOOT 👯

With pancakes served until you walk the plank, the Pannenkoekenboot takes you on a tour of the IJ lasting a good hour. You start in the old wooden harbour before heading past the central station to the islands in the harbour. *Daily, between 12.30pm and 5.45pm, exact times at amsterdam. pannenkoekenboot.nl | adults 17.50 euros, children 3–12 years 12.50 euros | departure from the NDSM quay | free ferry from the central station to the NDSM quay | Noord | ☲ 0*

SARAVANAA BHAVAN

A taste of the Indian subcontinent in the heart of Amsterdam. This restaurant is large, loud and always crowded. Dishes are served in authentic metal bowls. The menu is not limited to the usual suspects so it's a great

After a visit to the Rijksmuseum, grab a light supper at the Seafood Bar

opportunity to try new things. *Daily | Stadhouderskade 123 | tel. 020 7 53 12 | tram 4 Stadhouderskade | Zuid |* 🕮 *G6*

SEMHAR

Spicy Ethiopian dishes that you scoop up with a piece of flat bread instead of a knife and fork. Try a glass of banana beer or coffee with incense. *Daily | Marnixstraat 259–261 | tel. 020 6 38 16 34 | tram 5 Bloemgracht | Centrum |* 🕮 *E3*

THE SEAFOOD BAR

In this fish restaurant near Museumplein you can order a three-course meal as well as fish and chips and snacks – everything is fresh off the boat or from sustainable sources. *Daily | Van Baerlestraat 5 | tram 2, 3, 5, 12 Van Baerlestraat | Zuid |* 🕮 *E5*

WATERKANT

You won't find many locations more unusual – this cool bar and restaurant is nestled underneath the huge corkscrews of the Europarking multi-storey car park. It is popular in summer and serves Surinamese specialities alongside a good range of drinks. Delicious fish with cassava. *Daily | Marnixstraat 246 | waterkantamsterdam.nl | tram 5, 13, 17, 19 Elandsgracht | Centrum |* 🕮 *E4*

STREET FOOD

MAOZ FALAFEL

Maoz serves excellent crispy falafel balls in fluffy pitta bread. There is a self-service salad bar too. *Daily | Muntplein 1 | metro 52, tram 4, 14, 24 Rokin | Centrum |* 🕮 *G4 | further branches at Leidsestraat 85, Damrak 40*

TJIN'S

Cheap but delicious Surinamese sandwiches. You can get a beef roll with beans for 4 euros. *Daily | Van Woustraat 17 | tram 4 Stadhouderskade | Zuid |* 🕮 *G6*

VLAAMS FRIETHUIS VLEMINCKX

This stall sells Amsterdam's best chips. As a result there is always a long queue of expectant and hungry diners. Pick from 20 (!) types of mayonnaise. *Daily | Voetboogstraat 31 | tram 2, 11, 12 Koningsplein | Centrum |* 🕮 *F4*

SHOPPING

Amsterdam is a shopper's paradise. Everything is open seven days a week and both staff and customers remain friendly even when things are very busy.

The epicentre of the action is the triangle formed by Dam, Muntplein and Leidseplein. In the Kalvertoren and ☂ *Magna Plaza* shopping centres, you can hunt for bargains even when it rains. But what really makes Amsterdam attractive to shoppers is all the independent shops.

Sleek, stylish and sustainable – Sukha is a shop with modern values at its core

There is a cool mix of boutiques and pleasant cafés in the *9 straatjes* as well as in Utrechtsestraat and on the Haarlemmerdijk. Amsterdammers love using weekly markets for their food shopping and for buying everyday items. The Albert Cuyp market is the most famous – and is also a great spot for unusual souvenirs.

WHERE AMSTERDAM SHOPS

Westerpark

Van Hallstraat

OUD-

Browers-

JORDAAN

Nassaukade

Lindengracht

Westerstraat

Prinsengracht

Kostverlorenstraat

Hendrikstraat

NOORDERMARKT & LINDENGRACHT
Perfect for a Saturday food shop

S105

NEST

9 STRAATJES
Charming boutiques among international flagship stores

de Clerceqstraat

Nassaukade

Keizersgracht

Bilderdijkstraat

Leidsegracht

S100

Heinen Delftware ★

MARCO POLO HIGHLIGHTS

★ **ANTIQUARIAAT KOK**
Old books and prints as far as the eye can see ➤ p. 78

★ **BIJENKORF**
Traditional department store on the Dam ➤ p.79

★ **MARQT**
Supermarket stocking regional and organic products ➤ p. 82

★ **PUCCINI**
Handmade pralines with incredible ingredients ➤ p. 82

★ **ALBERT CUYPMARKT**
Multicultural outdoor market ➤ p. 83

★ **IJ-HALLEN**
Europe's largest flea market ➤ p. 84

★ **HEINEN DELFTWARE**
Genuine Royal Delftware and other hand-painted porcelain ➤ p. 85

Overtoom

S106

Eerste C. Huygenstraat

Overtoom

S100

Stadhouderskade

P. C. HOOFTSTRAA
For the bigger spenders:
Gucci, Prada & Co

Vondelpark

OUD-

Willemsparkweg

ZUID

IJ Hallen ★   NOORD

HEREN- & PRINSENSTRAAT
Small but perfectly formed, with everything from chocolate to clothes

KALVERSTRAAT & NIEUWENDIJK
Fashion chains to get teenagers' hearts racing

Bijenkorf ★

CENTRUM

Antiquariaat Kok ★

Puccini ★

PIEGELGRACHT
Antiques, art and oddities

Marqt ★

UTRECHTSESTRAAT
A perfect place to browse, with small boutiques and lovely cafés

Albert Cuypmarkt ★

400 m
437 yd

ANTIQUES

DE LOOIER

De Looier is the largest covered antiques market in the Netherlands. Its building on Lijnbaansgracht houses over 70 stalls and several shops, though some of the stands are not much bigger than a display case. They sell everything from porcelain to toys and furniture. On Saturdays, Sundays and Wednesdays, hobby dealers can rent a stall in the entrance area. *Elandsgracht 109 | tram 5, 7, 19 Elandsgracht | Centrum | ⫛ E4*

INSIDER TIP
Treasures among the tat?

EDUARD KRAMER

Antique Dutch tiles for every budget, from Baroque to Art Nouveau, from blue-and-white to colourful. *Nieuwe Spiegelstraat 64 | antique-tileshop. nl | Tram 1, 7, 19 Spiegelgracht | Centrum | ⫛ F5*

NEEF LOUIS

Strictly speaking, this shop situated in an old warehouse in Noord sells vintage furniture, not antiques. There are plenty of designer pieces (with a price to match) to be found among the old school desks and workshop lamps. *Papaverweg 46–48 | neeflouis.nl | bus 38 Klaprozenweg | Noord | ⫛ 0*

BOOKS

ANTIQUARIAAT KOK ★

This huge treasure-filled antiquarian bookshop is a paradise for bibliophiles. They also stock old maps and prints (sometimes already mounted). *Oude Hoogstraat 18 | kok.nvva. nl | metro 51, 53, 54 Nieuwmarkt | Centrum | ⫛ G4*

ATHENAEUM

One of the city's best-stocked bookshops, and the adjoining newsagent's has a huge range of magazines. *Spui 14–16 | tram 11, 12 Spui | Centrum | ⫛ F4*

BOEKENMARKT OUDEMANHUISPOORT

This book market is located in an 18th century arcade in the university quarter. *Oudemanhuispoort | metro 52 Rokin | Centrum | ⫛ G4*

WHERE TO START?

Amsterdam's most traditional shopping area is the **9 straatjes** (⫛ *E–F4*), nine little streets that run east–west between Westermarkt and Leidsegracht: Reestraat, Runstraat, Berenstraat etc. There are loads of little shops of various kinds, ranging from designer fashion to art books, and from junk to Dutch cheese – as well as lots of good cafés. The nearest tram stops for the *9 straatjes* are Westermarkt (tram 13, 17), Dam (tram 13,14) and Spui (tram 2, 11, 12).

The small independent shops on the *9 straatjes* put the fun back into shopping

CURIOSITIES

AMSTERDAM DUCK STORE
Rubber ducks everywhere you look in every costume you can imagine from Marilyn Monroe to the devil. Everything is possible! *Staalstraat 10 | metro 52, tram 4, 14, 24 Rokin | Centrum | ⊞ G4*

THE OTHERIST
Cases stuffed full of butterflies, glass eyes, old medical equipment and jewellery – *The Otherist* is a modern cabinet of curiosities with an incredible range. *Leliegracht 6 | otherist. com | tram 13, 17 Westermarkt | Centrum | ⊞ F3*

DEPARTMENT STORES

BIJENKORF ★
This department store, founded in 1870, is chic and expensive. Gucci etc. occupy the marble-clad ground floor, while on the upper floors you can find more affordable designer brands. *Dam 1 | tram 4, 14, 24 Dam | Centrum | ⊞ F3*

HEMA
What used to be a basic homeware store has become a kind of Dutch Ikea, were you can buy anything from toilet brushes and sofa cushions to baby clothes in sleek and minimalist designs. *E.g. in the Kalvertoren shopping centre | Kalverstraat/Heiligeweg | metro 52, tram 4, 14, 24 Rokin | Centrum | ⊞ F4*

HUDSON'S BAY
The exclusive Canadian chain has found itself a home in three buildings on the Rokin. *Rokin 21–49 | metro 52 Rokin, tram 4, 14, 24 Dam | Centrum | 🕮 F4*

FASHION & ACCESSORIES

HUTSPOT
If you are a fan of drainpipe jeans, oversized coats and classic-style racing bikes, you will love this concept store with its modern designer clothes and a hip café. *Rozengracht 204–210 | tram 13, 117 Marnixstraat | Centrum | 🕮 E4*

JAN
Designer bits and bobs, from handbags and jewellery to lifestyle books and accessories for the home. *Utrechtsestraat 74 | tram 4 Keizersgracht | Centrum | 🕮 G5*

JUTKA & RISKA
A little bit out of the way, but the 1970s and 1980s vintage fashion and accessories plus newer items designed by sisters Jutka and Riska Volkerts' own label make the trip more than worthwhile. *Bilderdijkstraat 194 | tram 3 Kinkerstraat, tram 5, 13, 17, 19 Bilderdijkstraat | West | 🕮 D4*

MARLIES DEKKERS
Flagship store of the "grande dame" of fashionable Dutch underwear. Simple but sexy lingerie is presented in luxurious fairy-tale surroundings. *Berenstraat 18 | tram 13, 14, 17 Westermarkt | Centrum | 🕮 F4*

NUKUHIVA
When you look at the basic clothes here you might not notice that this little boutique specialises in fairtrade fashion. Some of the profits go to educational projects in the developing world. *Haarlemmerstraat 36 | 10 mins walk from the main station | Centrum | 🕮 G2*

SISSY BOY
A Dutch fashion chain that also sells homeware, 👶 children's clothing and toys. *KNSM-laan 19 | tram 7 Azartplein | Oost | 🕮 L3*

SUKHA
Cool objects for your home, and fashion made from fine fabrics (with prices to match). This concept store's range is huge but everything is

Sissy Boy has a diverse range of cool urban design, from fashion to toys

homemade and has eco-credentials. *Haarlemmerstraat 110 | 10 mins walk from the main station |* *Centrum | ⫌ F2*

X BANK

This huge shop on the mezzanine floor of the W Hotel is stuffed full of Dutch design. Fashion, art and accessories are sorted by colour like a rainbow. Nothing is cheap, but you can browse for hours. *Spuistraat 172 | tram 13, 17 Dam | Centrum | ⫌ F3*

YDU – YOUNG DESIGNERS UNITED

Up-and-coming young designers can rent space on the racks here to sell their work. They guarantee that there are no more than four of each piece.

Keizersgracht 447 | tram 2, 11, 12 Keizersgracht | Centrum | ⫌ F4

FOOD & DRINK

Amsterdam shows how international it is in the many ⏿ *tokos* – small shops selling ingredients from all over the world. However, 🐖 Dutch supermarkets are also great places to stock up on a wide range of herbs and spices, and can be cheaper than other places in Europe. From lemongrass to cumin and fenugreek, the range is superb.

DE BIERKONING

The "Beer King" sells 2,000 different beers from all over the world, including obscure regional brews. *Paleisstraat 125 | bierkoning.nl | tram 2, 11, 12 Dam | Centrum | ⫌ F3*

JACOB HOOY & CO

Entering this spice shop is like taking a trip back in time. You'll find 500 kinds of herbs and spices, stored in wooden drawers and barrels labelled in gold lettering, filling the space with amazing aromas. Behind the counter there are 30 jars of drop – salty or sweet Dutch liquorice. *Kloveniersburgwal 10–12 | jacob-hooy. nl | metro 51, 53, 54 Nieuwmarkt | Centrum | ☐ G3*

KAASHUIS TROMP

Dutch and international cheese is piled to the rafters in this little shop on Utrechtsestraat. The staff are ready to help and will let you try before you buy. *Utrechtsestraat 90 | tram 4 Prinsengracht | Centrum | ☐ G5*

MARQT ★

A posh supermarket that only sells sustainable and regional products. Buy something to take home such as cheese, salty liquorice or beer from local breweries, or pick up a fresh pizza and salad to eat straight away. *Utrechtsestraat 17 | tram 4, 14 Rembrandtplein | Centrum | ☐ G4*

PUCCINI ★

Chocoholics will find themselves drooling over the selection at Puccini's. The chocolates are big and as unusual as they are delicious, with varieties blended with thyme, lemongrass and poppy seeds. *Staalstraat 17 | metro 51, 53, 54, tram 14 Waterlooplein | Centrum | ☐ G4*

It might be an idea to set a budget before going to Puccini's praline paradise

GALLERIES

GALERIE FONS WELTERS 🐷

A contemporary gallery showing mainly Dutch art – occasionally quite pretentious. *Bloemstraat 140 | fonswelters.nl | tram 5 Bloemgracht | Centrum | ₥ E3*

RON MANDOS GALERIE

One of the best-known galleries for contemporary international art. Sometimes it showcases a particular artist, other times it focuses on a particular subject. *Prinsengracht 282 | ronmandos.nl | tram 13, 17 Westermarkt | Centrum | ₥ E4*

HOMEWARES

DROOG@HOME

In the mid-1990s Droog Design made a name for itself with an experimental look. A few years ago, the designers' collective set up its own shop and gallery here. *Café Droog* is well hidden on the top floor but it is worth finding, especially during its high tea service in the afternoon (with unlimited refills). *Staalstraat 7b | droog.com | metro 51, 53, 54 Waterlooplein | Centrum | ₥ G4*

INSIDER TIP
Trendy tea and cake

FROZEN FOUNTAIN

Unconventional Dutch designs for everything from chairs to lamps. Nothing is off the peg, so the goods are priced accordingly. *Prinsengracht 645 | Tram 5, 7, 19 Elandsgracht | Centrum | ₥ F4*

WAAR

At Waar you can buy fair-trade food and also crockery, vases, baskets and bathroom accessories with modern and minimalist style. *Haarlemmderijk 57 | 10 mins walk from the main station | Centrum | ₥ F2*

JEWELLERY & DIAMONDS

AMSTERDAM VINTAGE WATCHES

This family business's motto is "pay more, buy less" and it makes sense with the kind of luxury vintage watches that they sell. They restore and service all their watches lovingly. *Singel 414 | amsterdamvintage watches.com | tram 2, 11, 12 Spui | Centrum | ₥ F4*

GASSAN DAM SQUARE

located if you need some gems in a rush. Apart from sparkling gemstones, you can pick up a high-end watch. *Rokin 1–5 | tram 4, 14, 24 Dam | Centrum | ₥ F3*

MARKETS

The best place to buy flowers and seeds is a 🐷 weekly market. The goods are half the price compared to the Singel Flower Market.

ALBERT CUYPMARKT ⭐

There truly is something for everyone at Amsterdam's biggest outdoor market and it is also gloriously multicultural. See, smell and buy vegetables, fish, cheese, spices and flowers, as well as Indian fabrics and

African cosmetics. There are plenty of street food stands with all kinds of cuisine from Surinamese sandwiches to Belgian waffles. It is busiest on a Saturday and can feel a bit sad on a Monday morning. *Mon–Sat 9.30am–5pm | metro 52 | tram 3, 12, 24 De Pijp | Zuid | ⌘ F-G6*

INSIDER TIP
Saturday is market day!

DAPPERMARKT 🐷

It might be less famous but it is no less culturally diverse (and is also a bit cheaper) than the Albert Cuypmarkt. In the city's trendy Oost district. *Mon–Sat 10am–4.30pm | Dapperstraat | tram 14 Pontanusstraat | tram 1, 3 Dapperstraat | Oost | ⌘ K5*

FLOWER MARKET

A gardener's paradise. A huge range of seeds and bulbs as well as cool houseplants and souvenirs – the prices are pretty punchy though. *Mon–Sat 9.30am–5pm | Singel 610–616 | metro 52 Rokin, tram 24 Muntplein | Centrum | ⌘ F4*

IJ-HALLEN ★

Once a month, half of Amsterdam makes a trip to Europe's biggest flea market in the NDSM shipyard, to bargain-hunt in massive warehouses filled with second-hand stuff. Find dates online. *Sat/Sun 9am–4.30pm | admission 5 euros | TT Neveritaweg 1 | ijhallen.nl | free ferry from the main station to the NDSM shipyard | Noord | ⌘ 0*

NOORDERMARKT

Every Monday a flea market gathers around the Noorderkerk, and on Saturday a food market occupies the same pitch. You can combine a stroll around the food market with a visit to the market on the adjoining Lindengracht. *Mon 9am–4pm flea market, Sat 9am–4pm organic produce | Noordermarkt and Westerstraat | tram 3 Marnixplein | Centrum | ⌘ F2*

WATERLOOPLEIN

The city's only daily flea market is on Waterlooplein. It sells everything imaginable, from bike tyres to incense burners and leather jackets. *Mon–Sat 10am–5pm | Waterlooplein | metro 51, 53, 54 Waterlooplein, tram 14 Mr. Visserplein | Centrum | ⌘ G4*

ANTONIA BY YVETTE

This tiny shop is literally floor-to-ceiling stuffed with every kind of slipper and clog you can imagine. In summer there are also flip-flops, and wellies in winter. *Gasthuismolensteeg 16 | tram 2, 11, 12 Spui | Centrum | ⌘ F4*

SHOEBALOO

The gleaming white interior of this shop is futuristic, and they sell shoes from luxury brands such as Prada. *Koningsplein 5 | tram 2, 11, 12 Koningsplein | Centrum | ⌘ F4*

UNITED NUDE

Dutch shoe design with a flair for eye-catching heels – designed by the nephew of the famous architect Rem

Koolhaas. *Spuistraat 125a | tram 2, 11, 12 Spui | Centrum | ⌂ F4*

SOUVENIRS

HEINEN DELFTWARE ★

Jaap and his son Joris paint some of the porcelain themselves, and they also sell products from the Royal Delft porcelain factory. On the second floor, you can watch porcelain painters at work. *Muntplein 12–14 | metro 52 Rokin, tram 24 Muntplein | Centrum | ⌂ G4*

INSIDER TIP
Watch artists at work

SPIEGEL

A souvenir shop that manages to avoid selling clogs or tulip bulbs. Instead, they sell a large range of cool accessories and trinkets made by Dutch designers. Prices range from good value to exorbitant. *Nieuwe Spiegelstraat 2a | tram 14, 24 Muntplein | Centrum | ⌂ F5*

TOBACCO

HAJENIUS

Tobacco, cigarettes and hand-rolled cigars have been sold since 1826 in the elegant interior of this long-established tobacconist's shop with its wood panelling and crystal chandeliers. You can even get them to roll your very own cigar in front of you. *Rokin 92 | metro 52, tram 4, 14, 24 Rokin | Centrum | ⌂ F4*

The Droog Collective has a reputation for witty design

GOING OUT

At the weekend, Amsterdam is a city that never sleeps. The centre buzzes all night long with busy outdoor bars and cafés. The hotspots for nightlife are Leidseplein and Rembrandtplein. Around Spui and Nieuwmarkt and in the De Pijp quarter, there are fewer tourists but equally vibrant scenes.

The traditional way to kick off the evening is a *borreluur*, when friends gather after work on a Thursday or Friday for beer and snacks

Traditional wood panelling and a lively atmosphere at In 'T Aepjen

There are lots of theatres for the culturally curious – even if most things are in Dutch. Music and dance can be enjoyed without the language barrier, but orchestras and ballet companies like the *Concertgebouw Orchestra* or *Nederlands Dans Theater* are in high demand, so book early to avoid disappointment. For louder beats, head to the clubs and gig venues. Some of these are housed in unconventional spaces like old churches or a skyscraper's basement.

WHERE AMSTERDAM GOES OUT

WESTERGASFABRIK
Dance in an old gas power station

MARCO POLO HIGHLIGHTS

★ **IN DE WILDEMAN**
The agony of choice: in this ancient *proeflokaal* (tasting room) you can try 200 kinds of beer ➤ p. 92

★ **EVENING CANAL TRIPS**
A unique experience: glide along the canals after dark ➤ p. 92

★ **TUSCHINSKI**
A fabulous old cinema – inside and out ➤ p. 93

★ **ESCAPE**
Huge club playing house music ➤ p. 94

★ **PARADISO**
Pop, rock and techno in a holy setting ➤ p. 95

★ **CONCERTGEBOUW**
One of the world's top orchestras benefits from superb acoustics ➤ p. 96

★ **HET MUZIEKTHEATER**
Something for every mood from experimental dance to grand opera ➤ p. 96

★ **STADSSCHOUWBURG**
Theatre on Leidseplein with an extensive programme ➤ p. 97

OUD ZUID
The bars west of the Concertgebouw are the smartest in the city

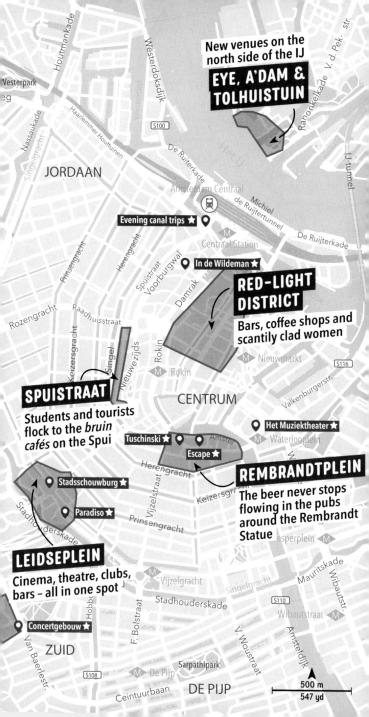

New venues on the north side of the IJ

EYE, A'DAM & TOLHUISTUIN

Vesterpark

Houtmankade

Westerdoksdijk

Kanonelkade V. d. Pek- str.

Haarlemmer Houttuinen

S100

Westerdoksdijk

De Ruiterkade

Het IJ

IJ-tunnel

Nassaukade

Singelgracht

JORDAAN

Amsterdam Centraal

Michiel de Ruijtertunnel

De Ruijterkade

Evening canal trips ★ 📍

Centraal Station Ⓜ

Prinsengracht

Herengracht

Keizersgracht

Spuistraat

Voorburgwal

In de Wildeman ★ 📍

Rozengracht

Raadhuisstraat

Singel

Nieuwezijds

Damrak

Rokin

RED-LIGHT DISTRICT

Bars, coffee shops and scantily clad women

Ⓜ Nieuwmarkt

S116

Ⓜ Rokin

Rokin

SPUISTRAAT

Students and tourists flock to the _bruin cafés_ on the Spui

CENTRUM

Valkenburgerstr.

📍 **Het Muziektheater ★**

Ⓜ Waterlooplein

Amstel

Tuschinski ★ 📍

Herengracht

Escape ★ 📍

Keizersgracht

REMBRANDTPLEIN

The beer never stops flowing in the pubs around the Rembrandt Statue

Stadhouderskade

Stadsschouwburg ★ 📍

Vijzelstraat

Prinsengracht

Paradiso ★ 📍

esperplein Ⓜ

LEIDSEPLEIN

Cinema, theatre, clubs, bars – all in one spot

Mauritskade

Wibautstr.

Vijzelgracht Ⓜ

Singelgracht

Stadhouderskade

S110

Wibautstraat Ⓜ

Amsteldijk

Concertgebouw ★ 📍

Hobbe

F. Bolstraat

V. Woustraat

Van Baerlestr.

ZUID

S108

Ⓜ De Pijp

Sarpathipark

DE PIJP

Ceintuurbaan

500 m
547 yd

BARS

APT.

This small but trendy cocktail bar shares the historic Odeon building on Singel with *Hoppa* brewery and the legendary *Supperclub*. Drinks are shaken and stirred until the small hours. *Sun-Wed 7pm-2am, Thu-Sat 7pm-4am | Singel 460 | tram 11, 12 Koningsplein | Centrum | ⊞ F4*

CAFÉ BRECHT

If Amsterdam has awakened your interest in Europe's cooler capitals, Café Brecht gives you an opportunity to try Berlin out without having to make another journey. Decked out like a Berlin bar and run by Germans, it is also a great place to watch live international football. *Sun-Thu 11am-1am, Fri/Sat 11am-3am | Weteringschans 157 | cafebrecht.*

WHERE TO START?

Amsterdam's **Leidseplein** *(⊞ E5)* is the beating heart of the city's nightlife. In the evening, this rather chaotic square bursts with life in its pubs, cinemas, theatres and clubs. The *Stadsschouwburg*, *Kino City* and the *De Balie* arts centre are all located on the square. Clubs such as *Jimmy Woo* and *Sugar Factory* are hidden away in the narrow streets around Leidseplein, and *Paradiso* and *Melkweg* are not far away. Trams 1, 2, 7, 11 and 12 stop at Leidseplein.

---

nl | tram 1, 7, 19, metro 52 Vijzelgracht | Centrum | ⊞ F5

DOOR 74

A speakeasy hidden behind an inconspicuous door just off the main drag of Rembrantplein. You have to reserve in advance. *Sun-Thu 8pm-3am, Fri/Sat 8pm-4am | Reguliersdwarsstraat 74 | tel. 06 34 04 51 22 | door-74. com | tram 4, 14 Rembrandtplein | Centrum | ⊞ G5*

MADAM

High up in the A'DAM tower, you can enjoy the best view of the city, accompanied by cocktails and dance music. *Daily from 9:30pm (and open as a restaurant earlier) | Overhoeksplein 3 | free ferry from the main station to Buiksloterweg | Noord | ⊞ G2*

NOL

A proper Jordaan bar with flowered wallpaper and crystal chandeliers. The regulars often sing along to Dutch hits played by the band. *Westerstraat 109 | tram 3 Marnixplein | Centrum | ⊞ F3*

W LOUNGE

The plush W Hotel has a trendy bar on its top floor with a beautiful view out over the city. But the crowning glory is the outdoor pool. You will be lucky to get a day of weather when you can swim in it, but it still adds to a vibe of chilled luxury if you sip a cocktail on its edge. *Daily until 1am, Fri/Sat until 2am | Spuistraat 175 | wamsterdam. com/wlounge | tram 2, 11, 12, 13, 17 Dam | Centrum | ⊞ F3*

You can try a wide variety of Brouwerij 't IJ's concoctions in their beer garden

CAFÉS & PUBS

During the week, most cafés and pubs are open until 1am and until 3am at the weekend.

BAR BOTANIQUE

The name reveals a lot – this Caribbean-inspired bar is decked out in plants. With a wide selection of wine and a young and international crowd, it has a great buzz. Live music (often) on Sundays. *Sun–Thu 9am–1am, Fri/Sat 9am–3am | Eerste Van Swindenstraat 581 | tram 14 Javaplein, tram 19 Eerste Van Swindenstraat | Oost | ⌑ K5*

BROUWERIJ 'T IJ

One of Amsterdam's few beer gardens is next to a historic windmill. The mill is home to the local T'IJ brewery, which makes 100% organic, unfiltered beer. On Fridays, Saturdays and Sundays they offer tours in English at 3.30pm. Tickets cost 6 euros and include a beer at the end. *Daily 2–8pm | Funenkade 7 | tram 7 Hoogte Kadijk | Oost | ⌑ K4*

INSIDER TIP
It's not only Heineken that does tours

DE CEUVEL

Dry-docked houseboats in the old shipyard are where lots of the city's creatives work. This café was furnished entirely from second-hand materials and serves organic food and local beers. Their parsnip *bitterballen* ("meatballs") are particularly worth trying. The café attracts a young and

INSIDER TIP
Vegetarian meatballs

alternative crowd, especially in summer. *Sun, Tue, Wed, Thu 11am–midnight, Fri/Sat 11am–2am | Korte Papaverweg 4 | metro 52 Noorderpark, bus 391, 394 Mosplein | Noord | ⊞ 0*

DE OOSTERLING 🚩

Traditional pub with a host of regulars, family-run for 100 years. Rustic wooden fittings, a good range of beers, no music. *Utrechtsestraat 140 | tram 1, 4, 7, 19 Frederiksplein | Centrum | ⊞ G5*

IN 'T AEPJEN

A proper old-school *bruin café* with well-worn wood panels and very few concessions to tourists. To top it all, the pub is found in one Amsterdam's oldest buildings dating from 1519. *Daily until 1am, Fri/Sat until 3am | Zeedijk 15 | 3 mins walk from the main station | Centrum | ⊞ G3*

IN DE WILDEMAN ★

This *proeflokaal* ("tasting room") is in an old distillery and looks like a cross between a pub and an old-fashioned pharmacy. Over 200 kinds of beer, 17 of them on draught. *Closed Sun | Kolksteeg 3 | tram 11, 12, 13, 17 Nieuwezijds Kolk | Centrum | ⊞ G3*

WYNAND FOCKINK 🚩

A tiny *proeflokaal* ("tasting room") dating from 1679, in a covered alleyway near the Krasnapolsky Hotel. A distillery that makes 60 kinds of schnapps is located behind it. The golden De Viif genever is matured in oak casks

INSIDER TIP
Liquid gold

for 5 years and has the same velvety flavour as good whisky. *Closes at 9pm! Daily | Pijlsteeg 31 | tram 4, 9, 16, 24 Dam | Centrum | ⊞ G4*

CANAL TRIPS

Glide along the ★ canals at night – what could be more romantic? The boat operated by *Rederij Lovers (daily, every 30 mins between 6pm and 10pm | 16 euros | Prins Hendrikkade 25–27, opposite the main station | tel. 020 5 30 10 90)* takes you on an hour's tour through the well-lit old city. Here and there you get a glimpse of the scene inside a houseboat at night.

SUPPERCLUB CRUISE

Supperclub Cruise offers a totally different kind of evening tour. This black boat slips out into Amsterdam's port and sometimes goes all the way out to the Ijsselmeer, with full-volume beats on board. It only returns to dock at 6 o'clock the next morning. *From 25 euros | De Ruijterkade 14 | by the northern exit from the main station | supperclubcruise.nl | Centrum | ⊞ G2*

CASINO

HOLLAND CASINO

A striking round building is home to one of Europe's most modern casinos. If you are over 18 and appropriately dressed, you can play roulette, blackjack, poker etc. beneath a colourful glass dome. *Daily from midday to 3am | admission 5 euros | Max Euweplein 62 | tram 1, 2, 7, 11, 12, 19 Leidseplein | Centrum | ⊞ E5*

CINEMAS

All films are shown in the original language with Dutch subtitles. Evening screenings usually start at 8pm and 10pm.

FC HYENA

A cinema and restaurant combo with sharing plates served from a hip open kitchen before diners head up to one of two screens to watch arthouse films. One screen has sofas instead of normal chairs. *Aambeeldstraat 24 | fchyena.nl | tel. 020 3 63 85 02 | bus 38 Hamerstraat, Fähre Oostveer: Zamenhofstraat | Noord | ⊞ K2*

THE MOVIES 🌂

Smaller than the Tuschinski and not as well known, but almost as beautiful, Amsterdam's oldest cinema on Haarlemmerdijk was opened in 1912. The auditorium and café-restaurant have Art Deco interiors. *Haarlemmerdijk 161 | tel. 020 6 38 60 16 | tram 3 Haarlemmerplein | Centrum | ⊞ F2*

TUSCHINSKI ★

When the King's mother, Beatrix, feels like going to the cinema, she sneaks out to the Tuschinski. And with good reason – it's a right royal treat because this movie palace, built in 1921, is an Expressionist architectural gem. Take a seat in its great auditorium or stroll

If Beatrix, the former Queen, goes to see a film, it's always at Tuschinski

through the foyer, and you'll feel like you've been transported back in time.

For real romance, book one of the boxes. For 42 euros you get a sofa for two and food and drink brought to you during the film. *Reguliersbreestraat 26 | tel. 0900 14 58 | tram 4, 14 Rembrandtplein | Centrum | ⌂ G4*

CLUBS

Amsterdam has a fairly laid-back clubbing scene: dress codes hardly exist, and bouncers are generally not a real problem, although you do sometimes have to wait to get in. If you really want to get into Amsterdam's clubbing scene, the *@Amsterdam Nightlife Ticket (amsterdamnightlifeticket.com)* is a worthwhile investment. For 10 euros you get entry to 20 clubs in a two-day period.

BITTERZOET

If you've had enough techno and electro, *Bitterzoet* is the place for you. Dance the night away to the sounds of jazz, soul and funk. Look out for gigs happening during the week. *Admission 10 euros | Spuistraat 2 | bitterzoet.com | tram 2, 11, 12, 13, 17 Nieuwezijds Kolk | Centrum | ⌂ G3*

CLUB AIR

A big club with electronic beats of the experimental kind. A prepaid system simplifies paying at the bar. *Amstelstraat 16 | air.nl | tram 4, 14 Rembrandtplein | Centrum | ⌂ C4*

DE SCHOOL

First, tuck into a three-, five- or seven-course menu before dancing it off to techno music in a former school on the outskirts of the city centre. The bouncers here are unusually strict and often refuse people. *Tue–Sat, times/admission depend on the event | Doctor Jan van Breemenstraat 1 | tel. 020 7 37 31 97 | deschoolamsterdam. nl | tram 13 Admiraal Helfrichstraat | Nieuw-West | ⌂ B4*

ESCAPE ★

One of the city's biggest clubs, accommodating up to 2,500 revellers. The biggest room, *The Club*, plays techno and house, with other floors offering a full range of genres. *Admission from 12 euros | Rembrandtplein 11–15 | escape.nl | tram 4, 14 Rembrandtplein | Centrum | ⌂ G4*

JIMMY WOO

Cool Chinese-influenced venue. Beneath more than 12,000 lamps, Amsterdam's young and beautiful crowd groove to house music on an enormous dance floor. You can chill out on black leather sofas surrounded by Chinese antiques in the lounge. *Admission from 10 euros | Korte Leidsedwarsstraat 18 | jimmywoo. com | tram 1, 2, 7, 11, 12, 19 Leidseplein | Centrum | ⌂ E5*

MELKWEG

Legendary arts centre in a converted dairy with a changing programme of concerts, club nights, films and exhibitions. *Café from 1pm, meals 6–9pm | admission 4–15 euros depending on*

Praise the music! Bands get a pretty special backdrop at Paradiso, housed in an old church

event | *Lijnbaansgracht 234* | *tram 1, 2, 7, 11, 12, 19 Leidseplein* | *Centrum* | 🗺 *E5*

PARADISO ⭐

This legendary dance club and gig venue housed in a converted church has been a fixture in Amsterdam's nightlife since the days of punk. Changing programme of events and techno DJs at weekends. In 2016 they opened a second branch in a cultural centre in Noord, where smaller and more experimental bands play. *Admission up to 20 euros* | *Weteringschans 6–8* | *paradiso.nl* | *tram 1, 2, 7, 11, 12, 19 Leidseplein* | *Centrum* | 🗺 *F5*

INSIDER TIP
A tiny piece of paradise

SHELTER

This is an underground club in the truest sense of the word. Located in the basement of the A'DAM tower, its underground entrance is not opened until after sundown. They play the full gamut of techno music. *Fri/Sat from 11pm* | *admission from 10 euros* | *Overhoeksplein 1* | *shelteramsterdam. nl* | *free ferry from the main station to Buiksloterweg* | *Noord* | 🗺 *G2*

SUGAR FACTORY

A small all-round club that is a venue for DJ sets but also hosts theatre productions and art performances. The musical offerings range from electro to jazz and world music. *Admission from 8.50 euros* | *Lijnbaansgracht 238* | *sugarfactory.nl* | *tram 1, 2, 7, 11, 12, 19 Leidseplein* | *Centrum* | 🗺 *E5*

WESTERUNIE

Every weekend Dutch DJs do their thing in a hall at the old Westergasfabrik (gasworks). The huge, 12-metre-high hall holds up to 800 revellers. *Klönneplein 4 | westerunie. nl | tram 5 Van Hallstraat | West | ☐ D1*

CONCERTS & BALLET

CONCERTGEBOUW ★

Amsterdam's concert hall is legendary and so are its acoustics. In the main auditorium, you really can hear a pin drop on the stage. There are 🐷 free lunch concerts every Wednesday at 12.30pm, to which lots of people come so get there early. *Concertgebouwplein 10 | tel. 0900 6 71 83 45 | concertgebouw. nl | tram 3, 5, 12 Museumplein | Zuid | ☐ E6*

HET MUZIEKTHEATER ★

When it was opened in 1986, this modern building on Waterlooplein was met with considerable scepticism. Over time, the people of Amsterdam have come to accept it because it gave them a new city hall as well as the only opera house in the Netherlands. Their name for the monumental edifice is *Stopera*, fusing "Stadhuis" (city hall) and "opera". In the foyer, free lunchtime concerts are held on Tuesdays at 12.30pm from Sept to May. *Waterlooplein 22 | tel. 020 6 25 54 55 | metro 51, 53, 54, tram 14 Waterlooplein | Centrum | ☐ H3*

INSIDER TIP
There is such a thing as a free lunch concert

MUZIEKGEBOUW AAN 'T IJ

The two halls of this glass-fronted waterside palace are mostly used for concerts of contemporary music. The walls, ceiling and floor of the halls are movable so that the acoustics can be perfectly tuned to every kind of music. *Piet Heinkade 1 | muziekgebouw. nl | tram 26 Muziekgebouw | Centrum | ☐ H3*

JAZZ CLUBS

BIMHUIS

Internationally renowned jazz venue, founded in 1974 and now housed in a spectacular new waterfront building. Mon–Wed jam sessions from 10pm. *Closed July and Aug | Piet Heinkade 3 | tel. 020 7 88 21 88 | tram 26 Muziekgebouw | Centrum | ☐ H3*

BOURBON STREET

Founded as a blues club in 1990, it has now broadened its musical range to take in everything from jazz to soul and funk. *Sun–Thu 10pm–4am, Fri/Sat until 5am | Leidsekruisstraat 6–8 | bourbonstreet.nl | tram 1, 2, 7, 11, 12, 19 Leidseplein | Centrum | ☐ E5*

JAZZCAFÉ ALTO

There are (usually free) live concerts in this tiny bar from 9pm every evening. A mix of up-and-coming and more established groups play all kinds of jazz, funk etc. Gets extremely full at the weekend. *Daily from 9pm | Korte Leidsedwarsstraat 115 | jazz-cafe-alto. nl | tram 1, 2, 7, 11, 12, 19 Leidseplein | Centrum | ☐ F5*

Much-loved club in a spectacular building: watch jazz on the waterfront at Bimhuis

THEATRES

BOOM CHICAGO
Founded in 1993 by a couple of American comedians, Boom Chicago has become a real institution in Amsterdam. The comedy often takes a critical look at politics and current affairs. *In the Rozentheater | Rozengracht 117 | tel. 020 4 23 01 01 | boomchicago.nl | tram 13, 117 Marnixstraat | Centrum | ▥ E3*

STADSSCHOUWBURG ★
This grand theatre with its ornate Neo-Renaissance façade opened in 1894 on Leidseplein. Its stage is the setting for major productions of classic drama in Dutch such as works by Ibsen and Chekhov. In summer, it plays host to many international performances during the Holland Festival. *Leidseplein 26 | stadsschouw burgamsterdam.nl | tram 1, 2, 7, 11, 12 Leidseplein | Centrum | ▥ E5*

ACTIVE & RELAXED

Cycling around Amsterdam is a pleasure – and good exercise!

SPORT & WELLNESS

IN & ON THE WATER

Not many people know that you can go windsurfing in central Amsterdam. Unfortunately, you have to head out to the Ijsselmeer rather than being on the canals. Book a private, three-hour beginner's course for 125 euros or a group course for 50 euros at *Surfcenter IJburg (May–Oct Wed, Thu, Fri 2pm–sunset, Sat/Sun 11.30am–6.30pm | reservations only by emailing info@surfcenterijburg.nl | surfcenterijburg.nl | tram 26 IJburg, then 5 mins walk | Oost | ▢ 0).*

If you'd rather put your faith in your own strength than in the wind, you can hire 👥 pedalos from *Stromma (10 euros/pers. for 1 hr, 15 euros/pers. for 1½ hrs | short.travel/ams10 | Centrum)* and explore the canals by yourself. They throw in a poncho if it's raining and they have bases at the *Rijksmuseum (Stadhouderskade 520),* on *Leidseplein (Stadhouderskade 11)* and at the *Anne Frank Huis (Prinsengracht 279).*

For swimming it is hard to beat the *Zuiderbad (Mon 7am–6pm, Tue 7–11am, midday–10pm, Wed 7–9am, midday–10pm, Thu 7–10.30am, 7–10pm, Fri 7am–10pm, Sat 8am–3pm, Sun 1–3.15pm | admission 3.75 euros | Hobbemastraat 26 | tram 2, 5, 12 Rijksmuseum | Zuid | ▢ F6).* Not much has changed there since 1912 when it was built – even the original changing cubicles are still in use. Two lanes are reserved for faster swimmers on weekday mornings.

NEW DIMENSIONS OF FUN 👥

Everything is a bit bigger than it should be in Amsterdam's indoor playground, *Tunfun (Wed–Sun 10am–6pm | admission adults 2.50 euros, children up to 18 years 8.50 euros | Meester Visserplein 7 | tram 14 Meester Visserplein | Centrum | ▢ H4).*

Jog through empty streets – if you start very early

From models of toy diggers to its maze and slides, it is literally a larger-than-life experience.

SPAS & WELLNESS

The furnishings at *Sauna Déco (Mon, Wed–Sat midday–11pm, Tue 3–11pm, Sun 1–7pm | admission from 19 euros | Herengracht 115 | tel. 020 6 23 82 15 | saunadeco.nl | tram 2, 11, 12, 13, 17 Nieuwezijds Kolk | Centrum | ▢ F3)* come from a Parisian department store which was torn down in the 1920s. The atmosphere is luxurious and stylish and they offer a full range of treatments from massages to manicures alongside a lounge for relaxing.

The Hotel Jakarta's pool, gym and sauna can be used by non-residents. The view from the pool in their *Wellcome Wellness* spa *(daily 7am–10pm | pool 12 euros, with sauna 17.50 euros | jakarta.*wellcomewellness.nl | Javakade 766 | tram 26 Kattenburgerstraat | Oost | ▢ J2)* is superb for looking out over the ships on the IJ.

WATCHING FOOTBALL

Ajax (with their distinctive red and white shirts) play their home games in the *Johann Cruiff Arena (Arena Blvd 1 | metro 50, 54 Strandvliet/ Arena | johancruijffarena.nl, ajax. nl | Zuidoost | ▢ 0)* in the south-east of the city. The gigantic stadium looks like a spaceship in the middle of a field and has space for 50,000 spectators under a retractable roof. You can get tickets for Ajax home games online, in the shop at the stadium or at Ticket Box sales outlets (usually kiosks and newsagents). You can also take a guided tour of the stadium *(daily, every 30 minutes between 10am and 4.30pm | 16.50 euros).*

FESTIVALS & EVENTS

APRIL

★ 🚩 **Koningsdag:** On 27 April the country celebrates King's Day. Until 2013, the Dutch honoured their Queen on 30 April every year. With the coronation of Willem-Alexander, this public holiday was moved to his birthday on 27 April. To celebrate, the whole of Amsterdam turns into one giant flea market, hordes of Dutch beer drinkers in orange T-shirts crowd the streets, and a big open-air concert is held on Museumplein. If 27 April falls on a Sunday, the celebrations take place on Saturday 26 April.

MAY

Bevrijdingsfestival: the liberation from German occupation in the Second World War is commemorated on 5 May with an all-day open-air festival on Museumplein. *4en5mei amsterdam.nl*

JUNE

Open Tuinen Dagen: every year on the third weekend in June, 30 canal gardens open their doors to visitors. *opentuinendagen.nl*

Holland Festival: a two-week event at which dance and theatre groups from all around the world set up shop in Amsterdam. The main venue is the Stadsschouwburg theatre on Leidseplein. *hollandfestival.nl*

JULY

Roots Festival: a vibrant array of world music bands perform in different venues around the city for ten days. The festival concludes with a free open-air concert in Oosterpark. *amsterdamroots.nl*

Amsterdam Pride: spectacular LGBTQ parade on the last weekend in July or the first weekend in August. *pride.amsterdam*

Amsterdam Pride – the city's most colourful party, with a boat parade on the canals

AUGUST

Grachtenfestival: the cultural highlight of the Amsterdam summer. The event that really draws the crowds is the free ★ **Prinsengrachtkoncert** by the Pulitzer Hotel in mid-August. *grachtenfestival.nl*

🦅 **Pluk de Nacht:** ten-day open-air film festival at the Stenen Hoofd on the banks of the IJ. *plukdenacht.nl*

SEPTEMBER

Open Monumentendag: an open day for almost all the historic buildings in the city takes place on the second Saturday of the month. *openmonumentendag.nl*

OCTOBER

Grachtenrace: rowing regatta on the canals on the second Saturday of the month. *grachtenrace.com*

TCS Amsterdam Marathon: the route takes in many of the city's sights and attracts around 45,000 participants. Third Sunday in October. *tcs amsterdammarathon.nl*

Amsterdam Dance Event: 2,000 international DJs visit the city each year for a four-day festival of techno, electro, house and hip-hop music. DJ sets and concerts in the evenings. *amsterdam-dance-event.nl*

NOVEMBER

Sinterklaas: St Nicholas arrives by boat on the third Sunday in November at the maritime museum and then mounts a horse to ride on to the Dam. *sintinamsterdam.nl*

DECEMBER

Pakjesavond: on 5 December it's "Package Eve". Traditionally, the Dutch exchange presents on this day and not on Christmas Day. Most museums close at 3pm and the streets are empty.

SLEEP WELL

SWEET SUITES

Amsterdam has lots of mechanical bridges which used to be operated from small bridge houses. Technology has rendered them obsolete and, until recently, they were often left empty. Until *Sweets Hotel (28 rooms | tel. 020 740 10 10 | sweetshotel.amster dam | €€€)* began converting them into small hotel suites – and there are now 28 in operation. The "hotel" is spread across the city but each room has space for two people and can boast an unbeatable canalside location. Breakfast can be provided on request. The best (and in highest demand) room is number 103 which is just 10 minutes from the city centre despite being in a park.

INSIDER TIP
A greener spot

DEPOT DREAMS

Housed in a former tram depot, the 55 rooms at the *Hotel de Hallen*

(Bellamyplein 47 | tel. 020 8 20 86 70 | hoteldehallen.com | tram 7, 17 Ten Katestraat | €€ | West | ᗑ D4) have been fitted around the building's historical elements, and sit around a comfortable central foyer with interesting art. A perfect place to chill out. The Foodhallen (p. 62) is right next door.

MINIATURE REALM

A boiler house from 1897 that used to belong to the waterworks now houses Amsterdam's smallest hotel – *De Windketel. (Watertorenplein 8c | info@ windketel.nl | windketel.nl | tram 5 Van Hallstraat | €€€ | West | f D2).* The single two-person suite is furnished with pieces by Dutch designers and is spread over three floors.

INDUSTRIAL REGENERATION

A total of three five-star suites can be found at the *Faralda Kranhotel (NDSM-Plein 78 | tel. 020 7 60 61 61 |*

A five-star suite in an old crane – only in Amsterdam

faralda.com | free ferry to the NDSM shipyard from the main station | Noord | 🕮 0), situated in a former crane in the NDSM shipyard. Two panoramic lifts take you to the jacuzzi, where you can relax at a height of 50m. VIPs and international DJs are among those who appreciate touches like this and pay the high tariff.

HOTEL? NO THANKS!

Are hotel rooms too conventional for you? How about spending the night in an old tram, or behind a secret door hidden in a bookcase, or in a house within a house? The 🦇 affordable rooms in Hotel Not Hotel (23 rooms | Piri Reisplein 34 | tel. 020 8 20 45 38 | hotelnothotel.com | tram 7, 17 Witte de Withstraat | € | West | 🕮 C4) are spread out throughout a large communal living space. They also have a cocktail bar named (for unfathomable reasons) after the actor Kevin Bacon.

TAILORED TO TASTE

The Exchange (Damrak 50 | tel. 020 5 23 00 80 | hoteltheexchange. com | tram 4, 14, 24 Dam | €€ | Centrum | 🕮 G3) is just the right place for fashionistas. All of the hotel's 61 rooms have been "dressed" in an original way by graduates of the Amsterdam Fashion Institute. If you feel inspired by your surroundings, you can also give it a go, because each room has a sewing machine.

SLEEK SLEEP SHIP

It would be hard to find more classic accommodation than the Levant B&B (Levantkade 90 | levantbb.nl | bus 65 Levantplein | €€ | Havens-Oost | 🕮 L3), a decommissioned barge in the eastern harbour district. The large cabin is fitted out for two guests and has its own bathroom.

DISCOVERY TOURS

Want to get under the skin of the city? Then our discovery tours provide the perfect guide – they include advice on which sights to visit, tips on where to stop for that perfect holiday snap, a choice of the best places to eat and drink, and suggestions for fun activities.

Rijksmuseum: ultra-modern art on the outside and Golden Age art on the inside

DISCOVERY TOURS

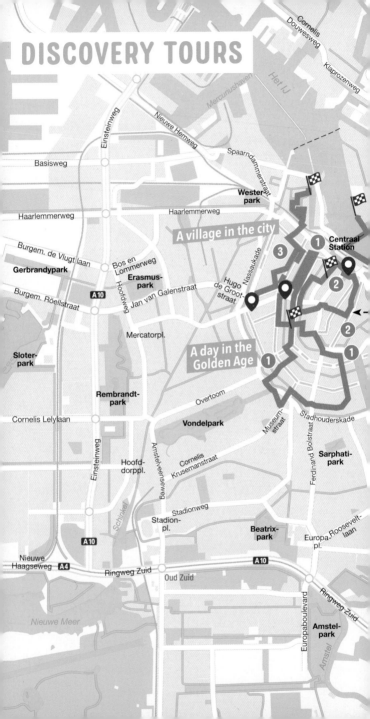

A village in the city

Centraal Station

A day in the Golden Age

Westerpark

Gerbrandypark

Erasmuspark

Hugo de Grootstraat

Sloterpark

Rembrandtpark

Mercatorpl.

Vondelpark

Cornelis Lelylaan

Hoofddorppl.

Stadionpl.

Beatrixpark

Sarphatipark

Overtoom

Cornelis Krusemanstraat

Stadionweg

Nieuwe Haagseweg

Ringweg Zuid

Oud Zuid

Ringweg Zuid

Nieuwe Meer

Europaboulevard

Amstelpark

Basisweg

Einsteinweg

Nieuwe Hemweg

Spaarndammerstraat

Haarlemmerweg

Burgem. de Vlugt laan

Bos en Lommerweg

Hoofdweg

Jan van Galenstraat

Burgem. Röellstraat

Nassaukade

Museumstraat

Ferdinand Bolstraat

Stadhouderskade

Einsteinweg

Amstelveenseweg

Schinkel

Europapl.

Roosevelt-laan

Amstel

Mercuriushaven

Het IJ

Cornelis Douwesweg

Klaprozenweg

❶ A DAY IN THE GOLDEN AGE

➤ See the Canal Ring from every angle
➤ Get up close to Rembrandt and pals
➤ Eat and drink like it's the 17th century

📍 Westermarkt   🏁 Westermarkt

🔄 8.5km   🚶 1 day (2 hrs total walking time)

ℹ️ ❸ **Westertoren**: admission 8 euros
❺ **Het Grachtenhuis**: admission 15 euros
❼ **Rijksmuseum**: admission 17.50 euros

A LATE BREAKFAST WITH A VIEW

❶ Westermarkt

Amsterdammers are not early risers and so an ideal day does not begin before 10am with breakfast in a place near the ❶ Westermarkt. *Head north for a bit on the west side of the Keizersgracht. Turn left down the Leliegracht and cross the bridge at the end to get to the west side of the Prinsengracht. Continue heading north past the next bridge, then look to your left where you will find* the very traditional ❷ Café t'Smalle *(Egelantiersgracht 12)*. It has not retained all its original 18th-century features but its small, sunny terrace on the canal is like a box at the theatre in summer. The next destination can be seen from here too: the unmistakable ❸ Westertoren ➤ p. 40, which *towers above the other side of the Prinsengracht.* If you climb up this church tower – the highest in Amsterdam – you will be rewarded with a wonderful view of the almost-entirely-preserved historic city centre.

❷ Café t'Smalle

❸ Westertoren

CANALS, CANALS, CANALS

❹ Grachtenring

Once you are back at ground level, it's time to explore the ❹ Grachtenring ➤ p. 39. *Head past the Westerkerk and turn right before taking the next left to reach the* Keizersgracht. The canal is lined by a row of elegant 17th-century grand houses, and thanks to the

legendary *lack of curtains* ➤ p. 25, you can have a peek at some of the marbled interiors with their stucco ceilings. *Head north along the canal.* Most of the canal houses have simple brick façades, but every now and then you will come across something different, such as the "House with Heads" (Keizersgracht 123), whose façade is adorned with the busts of Greek gods. *Continue northwards until you reach the Brouwersgracht,* which is surrounded by former brewery warehouses, *then turn right. Cross over the small but pretty pedestrian bridge to get to the* Herengracht, *which is the most stylish of the three main canals. Stroll southwards* until you come across Huis Bartolotti, which sits on a bend in the canal and appears to have a curved façade. But this is an optical illusion – the building's

INSIDER TIP
A concave canal house

grand Renaissance ornamentation gives it the impression of gently curving around what is in fact a hard break between its two halves. *Head on for 10 minutes until you get to the* ❺ Grachtenhuis ➤ p. 41, which tells the story of the Grachtenring's construction.

❺ Het Grachtenhuis

GET SOME GRUB BEFORE INDULGING IN SOME ART

It will be getting on for midday by now and your stomach is probably rumbling. *Walk just a bit further south and turn right at the next corner onto the snug Leidsegracht, then head left on the Keizersgracht to get to the charming café* ❻ Morlang ➤ p. 62, which has a waterside terrace. After a bite to eat, hop aboard *tram no. 2 or 5 at the stop on Keizersgracht and head off to the* ❼ Rijksmuseum ➤ p. 52. From the modern foyer head back in time to the Golden Age for a few hours by exploring the museum's stunningly beautiful galleries where you can admire masterpieces by Rembrandt and his contemporaries, as well as a small but perfectly formed collection of Asian art.

❻ Morlang

❼ Rijksmuseum

THE CALL OF THE SHOPS & A DARKLY BEAUTIFUL CINEMA

If you need a breath of fresh air after taking in the paintings, grab a bench in the museum's gardens and watch the kids playing happily in the fountains. *Afterwards, head north through the pedestrian tunnel and cross Museumbrug to Weteringsschans. From the tram stop Spiegelgracht, take tram number 7 or 10 to Frederiksplein.* You'll need to keep an eye on your cash here, but not because of pickpockets: opposite the park to your left, ❽ Utrechtsestraat stretches to the north, lined with lots of little shops and cafés. Taste some home-made chocolate in Chocolaterie Van Soest *(no. 143),* and shop for some designer clothes at Look Out *(no. 91)* or gifts at Jan ➤ p. 80 *(no. 74).* At the end of Utrechtsestraat, you will find bustling Rembrandtplein.

❽ Utrechtsestraat

Old-school interior with an airy canalside exterior: breakfast at Café t'Smalle

From the north-west corner of the square, head down Reguliersbreestraat, which will take you to Muntplein. Have a look into the foyer of the cinema ❾ Tuschinski ➤ p. 93, with its gorgeous dark Art Deco interior. *Leave Muntplein and head to the Rokin, then turn left onto the Spui. Behind the inconspicuous wooden door within the white façade on the right-hand side of the square,* the ❿ Begijnhof ➤ p. 37 awaits. This somewhat hidden oasis in the midst of all the shopping streets has a quiet period shortly before it closes at 5pm.

	❾ Tuschinski
	❿ Begijnhof

AN AFTER-WORK BEER & A GENEVER BEFORE BED

Afterwards, join the Amsterdammers for *borreluur* (post-work drinks) – try strong beer from the local *Brouwerij 't IJ* in the historic pub ⓫ Café Hoppe ➤ p. 38, located on the *western side of the Spui*. If you want to go Dutch on a meal, go *a few metres further*

⓫ Café Hoppe

north on Spuistraat to the restaurant ⑫ D'Vijff Vlieghen ➤ p. 64. *After your meal, head north along the street and then turn left onto Raamsteeg. Cross over Singel, Herengracht and Keizersgracht, and then turn right down the Prinsengracht.* ⑬ Proeflokaal der Destille A. van Wees *(Herengracht 319)* awaits, where you can round off your day with a shot of genever while enjoying a view over the canal. Return to the start of the day's tour at the ① Westermarkt.

② TASTY AMSTERDAM

➤ A taste of China in Amsterdam
➤ Eating herring like the Dutch
➤ Spoilt for choice: chocolate or cheese?

📍 Centraal Station

🏁 Centraal Station

↻ 4km

🚶 Half a day (1 hr's total walking time)

ⓘ Bring a big appetite on this tour because it crosses through the Wallen, stopping at one fine food shop after the other. It is best to plan it for an afternoon to ensure most of the establishments are open.

CLASSY COFFEE TO KICK THINGS OFF

As a trading city, food has always played a key role in Amsterdam's history. About 700 years ago, when the city's first residents built a dam to join the banks of the Amstel, a bustling market soon appeared where fishermen from near and far sold their wares. Goods from around the world were shipped over river and sea to Amsterdam and sold in the harbour. This market was located exactly where the ① Centraal Station ➤ p. 30, Amsterdam's main station, stands today – and *it also marks the beginning of this walking tour. From the square in front of the station, head south and turn left*

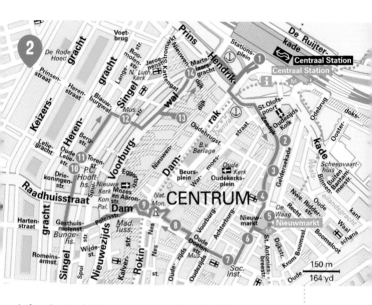

before the Hotel Victoria to get to the tip of Zeedijk. To get off to a good start, enjoy a lovely cup of coffee in the cosy ❷ Hofje van Wijs *(Zeedijk 43)*. This coffee and tea shop was founded in 1792 and is the royal family's favoured supplier. The Dutch love their coffee – annual per-capita consumption of roasted bean juice is around 150 litres.

❷ Hofje van Wijs

IN THE MIDDLE OF CHINATOWN

With your energy level up, *take a walk along the Zeedijk.* You will soon notice Chinese shops and street signs as you have now arrived in Amsterdam's Chinatown ➤ p. 33. On the corner of Stormsteeg, pop into ❸ Toko Dun Yong, one of the oldest Asian shops in the city. This

❸ Toko Dun Yong

INSIDER TIP
Family-run feast

family-owned shop first opened its doors in 1959. Asian food is stacked on the shelves on the ground floor, while woks, steam baskets and other items can be found on the three upper storeys. In the evening, *cooking workshops (cooking.dunyong.com)* are held on the first floor.

FINALLY, SOME FISH!

Continue on the Zeedijk past windows filled with Peking ducks and colourful rice cakes. Just when you feel like you are really in Hong Kong or Shanghai, you will stumble across the *tiny shop at number 129*, ❹ Viswinkel Zeedijk, which sells tasty smoked fish and particularly good Dutch pickled herring (*maatjes*). The herring trade was an important part of Amsterdam's economy from the very beginning and street names such as *Haringpakkerssteeg* or *Zoutsteeg* ("salt quay") still bear witness to this. Even if you are not a fan of oily fish, you should give the herring a try here. According to true connoisseurs, the pickles and onions usually served with *maatjes* actually mask the true taste of the fish and should be left out.

HERBS & SPICES

For centuries there has been a daily market on the Nieuwmarkt ➤ p. 33. The stalls cluster around ❺ De Waag ➤ p. 33, which was once part of the city gate and served as the official weigh house from 1618 onwards. Merchants had their wares weighed on the calibrated scales to make sure that they were not being cheated when they bought grain or cheese. Today, the building is surrounded by cafés and pubs as well as small delis, ice-cream shops, street food stands and ❻ Jacob Hooy & Co ➤ p. 82, a herb specialist with a long history. The Dutch East India Company brought all manner of herbs and spices to the city from an early period, and the company's former headquarters was *located around the corner in* ❼ Oost-Indisch Huis, which you can get to by *walking a short way along Kloveniersburgwal and then turning right onto Oude Hoogstraat*. Have a look at the lovely courtyard of this building designed by the architect Hendrick de Keyzer.

JUNIPER JUICE FROM A DOLL'S HOUSE

Continue walking down the busy streets Oude Hoogstraat and Damstraat until you reach Oudezijds Voorburgwal. Take a right and then an immediate left and you will find yourself in the narrow Pijlsteeg, where the tiny emporium of ❽ Wynand Fockink ➤ p. 92

❹ Viswinkel Zeedijk

❺ De Waag

❻ Jacob Hooy & Co

❼ Oost-Indisch Huis

❽ Wynand Fockink

hides at the end of the road. Give their *Superior Genever* a try. Your glass will be poured to the brim so you will probably have to bend down and slurp the first few sips. Your mood lightened, *continue on to* ❾ Dam, a square which was home to the fish market in the 16th century – freshwater fish were sold on the east side and saltwater fish on the west. To the left, you will see Rokin's harbour. A bit further along, the shopping street Kalverstraat runs into the square where calves were once driven to the livestock market.

❾ Dam

WHATEVER YOUR HEART DESIRES: CHOCOLATE, CHARCUTERIE OR BEER

Leave the Koninklijk Paleis ➤ p. 35 *to the right behind you and follow Paleisstraat to the former city moat called Singel, where you should turn right. Opposite the Torensluis bridge, at Singel 184, a true temptation awaits at* ❿ Puccini ➤ p. 82 *whose designer pralines with interesting flavours confirm that the Dutch still love to experiment with spices. If you are more in the mood for something savoury, then head a few doors down to* ⓫ Reypenaer *(Singel 182).* This cheese shop

❿ Puccini

⓫ Reypenaer

Herb paradise: at Jacob Hooy & Co you will be taken back in time

sells fine cheeses naturally ripened in an old warehouse near Utrecht and offers regular tastings *(Mon/Tue 1pm, 3pm; Wed–Sun noon, 1.30pm, 3pm, 4.30pm)*. Once you've finished gorging, *continue along the canal to the north and then turn right at the first bridge onto the narrow Lijnbaanssteeg* ⑫ **Van Dooren**. Try their salami seasoned with nutmeg and cloves as a nod to the country's colonial past. Of you fancy washing it down with a local beer from a brewery like *Brouwerij 't IJ*, head on to ⑬ **In de Wildeman** ➤ p. 92. To get to the pub, *head north along Nieuwezijds Voorburgwal for a bit, then turn right onto Nieuwezijds Kolk. The pub is hidden a few metres behind a small picturesque house, built in 1620, that belonged to the Kornmessergilde (corn appraisers' guild).* From the outside, you wouldn't guess that this small tavern has 18 draught beers and more than 250 types in bottles.

More than enough choice – there are over 200 types of beer at In de Wildeman

⑫ Van Dooren
⑬ In de Wildeman

VENDING VICTUALS

From here, follow Nieuwezijds Voorburgwal to get back to the start of the day's tour. Have you had enough of all the haute cuisine you've been sampling and want something more down-to-earth? Then head to the *corner of Nieuwendijk* where you will find the famous (or rather infamous) ⑭ **Automatiek FEBO** *(Nieuwendijk 50))*. Put some coins in or scan your card and pull out a piping hot croquette, then stroll back to the ❶ **Centraal Station**.

⑭ Automatiek FEBO

❶ Centraal Station

❸ A VILLAGE IN THE CITY

➤ Explore the Jordaan
➤ Restaurants and retail therapy near the Noordermarkt
➤ Escape the masses on the western harbour islands

📍 The corner of Lijnbaansgracht/Rozengracht

🏁 De Gouden Reael

→ 4km

🚶 Half a day (1 hr's total walking time)

ℹ Tram 5, 13, 17 Marnixstraat/Rozengracht to the starting point

THE ALMS HOUSE OF AMSTERDAM

Begin your walking tour at the point where the ❶ Lijnbaansgracht meets Rozengracht *and head north along the canal.* In the past, ropes were made alongside this very long canal, which used to lie just outside the city walls. Rembrandt himself was charmed by this artisans' quarter where he set up his studio in a warehouse on ❷ Bloemgracht in 1637. *To find this, turn right on the second corner you reach.* In the Jordaan district, everything is a bit smaller and cosier than along the canal ring. Quaint houses snuggle up to each other while little bridges span the tree-lined canals. When you walk past the houses at 87 to 91, you will find three well-preserved, identical stepped gable houses from the 17th century. *At the end of the Bloemgracht, turn left down 1e Leliedwarsstraat*, which is home to modern houses as well as ones dating back to the Golden Age. In the 19th century, Jordaan became a kind of alms house for Amsterdam's poor. Many of the old buildings fell into ruin and had to be replaced by newly constructed houses in the 1980s, after earlier 1960s plans to pull down much of what was left were thankfully discarded. Nowadays, this quarter is once again a popular place to live, which has something to

❶ Lijnbaansgracht/ Ecke Rozengracht

❷ Bloemgracht

do with the many nice cafés, galleries and shops that line its streets. If you like to browse small, characterful shops, this is the place for you. For example, *head across the Egelantiersgracht and keep walking straight on until you stumble upon the nostalgic* ❸ Oud-Hollandsch Snoepwinkeltje *(2e Egelantiersdwarsstraat 2)*, with its shelves full of old-style Dutch sweets.

❸ Oud-Hollandsch Snoepwinkeltje

THE BEST APPLE CAKE

Continue by heading along Tuinstraat, then turn left down Prinsengracht until you reach the ❹ Noorderkerk ➤ p. 39, the main Protestant church in Jordaan. If you are already getting hungry, try a piece of Dutch apple cake (*appeltaart*) on Noordermarkt ➤ p. 84 at ❺ Winkel 43 or, if it is Saturday, buy a snack at the organic farmer's market. *Afterwards, keep going north, cross the Lekkeresluis bridge and have a look at houses 85–133.* Here you will find the picturesque ❻ Van Brienenhofje *(Mon–Fri 6am–6pm, Sat 6am–2pm).* These *hofjes* were houses funded by merchants as residences for low-income elderly people living on their own. Today, there are still 46 of these hidden oases with their lovingly tended courtyards located in Jordaan.

❹ Noorderkerk

❺ Winkel 43

❻ Van Brienenhofje

INSIDER TIP
A courtyard oasis

COBBLES & CULTURE

Walk back across the same bridge and head towards the northwest along Brouwersgracht. Cross over the Oranjebrug to the right. A few minutes later, you will pass under the train tracks to get to Hendrik Jonkerplein. The western harbour islands – Bickerseiland, Prinseneiland and Realeneiland – can all be seen from here. Originally, all the factories or businesses that were too smelly and noisy for the civilised city centre were banished to these islands. Tar and salt works, ropemakers, shipyards and fish processing plants settled on the water's edge. Warehouses were built behind them and soon thereafter houses were put up for workers and seamen. Today, almost all of the former workshops have been turned into sought-after flats and artists' studios. *Cross over the square to*

7 Bickersgracht. Old brick houses, cobblestones and overgrown canal gardens lend this street a nostalgic charm. It is quite hard to believe that this area was considered one of the city's worst places to live in the 1960s. *On the other side of the canal, you can get to* **8 Prinseneiland** *by crossing a small bridge.* Galgenstraat means "Gallows Street", so named because the gallows that were located on the northern banks of the River IJ could be seen from here. The pretty warehouses that line the entire island conceal the morbid but now-disappeared history of this street. Their names such as De Windhond, De Teerton

7 Bickersgracht

8 Prinseneiland

Tulip season over? The Noordermarkt's sunflowers are just as photogenic

or De Witte Pelicaan are prettily illustrated on the gables or painted ornately on the shutters. *Follow the street on Prinseneiland clockwise and walk around the south side of the island.*

OVER THREE HERRINGS BRIDGE TO HOUSEBOATS & THE HARBOUR

At the northern end of the island, cross over the ❾ Drieharingenbrug *to get to* ❿ Realeneiland. This picturesque drawbridge was named after the house De Drie Haringen ("The Three Herrings") located on the other side of the canal. The Realengracht, whose banks are lined with small shipyards, is home to many bobbing houseboats converted from old freight barges. Right around the corner, you will find the quay called ⓫ Zandhoek, whose name comes from the sand market that was established on this spot in 1634. A row of impressive canal houses along this pier hint at the wealth of some of the merchants who once lived here. Inside the last house, ⓬ De Gouden Reael, you will find a lovely café with a sunny terrace on the waterfront. It is the perfect place to enjoy a glass of wine or a meal

❿ Realeneiland

⓫ Zandhoek

⓬ De Gouden Reael

at the end of the day's walk. When you are ready to head home, *cross the bridge behind the Gouden Reael and walk down the street to Westerdoksdijk. Just around the corner to the right, you will find the bus stop for No. 48 (to Borneo Eiland), which runs to the main station.*

❹ MODERN WATERSIDE ARCHITECTURE

➤ A bike trip to the harbour islands
➤ Scale Amsterdam's quirkiest bridge
➤ See how people build on the canals today

📍	Lloyd Hotel	🏁	Eye Film Institute
→	10km	🚲	Half a day (45 mins' cycling)
ℹ	Cost: bike hire around 12 euros		

WHERE WHALES GLISTEN IN THE SUN

The best way to explore Amsterdam's modern waterside architecture is in typical Dutch style with a bike (*rentals ➤ p. 130*). *Hop on and head to the* ❶ **Lloyd Hotel** (*Oostelijke Handelskade 34*). Originally built as a home for ex-pat employees by the Lloyd shipping company in 1918, it was reopened as a boutique hotel in 2005. Have a look at the surprisingly bright restaurant to get a sense of its new design. *From the IJ harbour on the opposite side*, you get a first glimpse of the islands and their new architecture. Across the water, you can see Java-Eiland with its myriad of urban residential buildings and KNSM-Eiland with its mix of large housing blocks and picturesque houseboats. Biking around the islands on a sunny day will reveal the charm of this diverse architecture. *Cycle in an easterly direction along the water.* The ❷ **Walvis ("Whale") apartment block** peeks outs from behind the white IJ tower, with its zinc façade glistening in the sun on a clear day. The

❶ Lloyd Hotel

❷ Walvis apartments

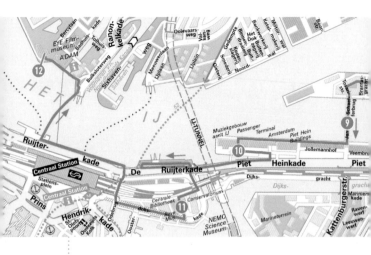

3 Sporenburg

3 Sporenburg peninsula with its low, dark-brick houses sits just behind these flats. The architects made a virtue out of necessity here because the new structures on the island had to be high density and low rise. What emerged was a new kind of house facing inwards with roof-top terraces and courtyards. Apart from flower-pots and benches, there are no gardens in front of these houses – the water from the harbour basin serves as a substitute for green space. Almost everyone who lives here owns a small boat.

WHERE RED SNAKES WRITHE
Cycle down Ertskade and JF van Hengelstraat, then circle around the head of the peninsula, where you will see the expressively curved, bright-red **4** Python Bridge that spans across the Spoorwegbassin to Borneo. Park your bike and climb up the bridge so that you can enjoy a panoramic view of the area. *Then continue along the Panamakade until your reach the second red bridge*, which is much lower and therefore bicycle friendly. *On the other side of the bridge, turn left and cycle around the head of the* Borneo peninsula where something rather special awaits. For the first time since the 17th century, the city has sold individual lots to private individuals, making the **5** Scheepstimmermanstraat unique in the

4 Python Bridge

5 Scheepstimmermanstraat

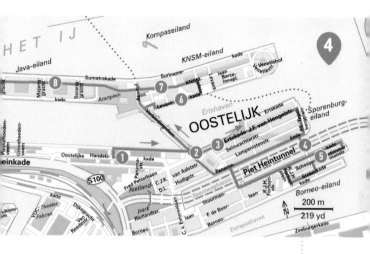

Netherlands. Buyers were allowed to build a terraced house designed by an architect of their choice so a great variety of styles is represented as a result. Biking along this street is like passing through a colourful gallery of architectural experiments. Particularly unusual examples include the house at number 120 which is built around a tree, and the house at number 62 which is clad entirely in wood. For the prettiest view of these houses, *look at them from the small pedestrian bridge to Stokerkade.*

INSIDER TIP
New take on terraced housing

ON THE ART OF LIVING
From here, head along Stokerkade, past a large brown block of flats and back over the bicycle bridge, then past the whale building until you get to the dam that leads across to KNSM, the island belonging to the Royal Dutch Shipping Company. It is dominated by the large, sculpture-like ⑥ Piraeus housing block designed by German architects Kollhoff and Rapp, which encircles the small old building to your right. If you need a little break, the café Kanis en Meiland in the Pireaus complex is a nice place to stop. From its waterfront terrace, you can watch the comings and goings on the decks of the houseboats docked in the harbour basin. If you are in the mood for some designer shopping, the

⑥ Piraeus apartments

shops in ❼ Loods 6 *directly on the KNSM-Laan to the north* are perfectly placed. At Sissy Boy ➤ p. 80 *(no. 19),* you will find fashion and accessories, while Pols Potten *(no. 39)* offers designer homeware and Imps & Elfs *(no. 297)* sells children's clothes and furnishings. *To the west of the dam, KNSM borders* ❽ Java-Eiland. The atmosphere on this island is more urban. Tall blocks line the busy street of Sumatra-Kai on the north side of the island. *Rather than following the cars, take the parallel path through the lovely and peaceful inland park until you cross left over the* ❾ Jan Schaeffer Bridge. It ends at the Oostelijke Handelskade beneath the old Wilhelmina Packing House – now a cultural centre. *Turn right from here and pedal along the fishtail-shaped cruise ship terminal to the* ❿ Muziekgebouw aan 't IJ ➤ p. 96, the striking glass concert hall built by Danish architects 3XN.

ACROSS THE WATER FOR A VIEW OF THE EYE

Cross the little bridge and turn onto the cycle path at the first set of lights on Ruijterkade. Cross the bridge and you will now be back on Oosterdokseiland. Have a look around the imposing ⑪ Centrale OBA ➤ p. 32, a superbly designed library. *Then continue along Oosterdokskade, heading right at the end of the peninsula beneath the train tracks, then left along the water. After a few hundred metres, you will reach the ferry terminal behind the main station. Hop aboard the free ferry that heads to Buiksloterweg to get to the north shore*, where the futuristic ⑫ Eye Film Institute ➤ p. 54 marks the end of the tour around 1pm. Give your legs a little rest and have lunch on the waterfront terrace or in its spectacular foyer.

⑪ Centrale OBA

⑫ Eye Film Institute

Like the serpent of the same name, the bright red Python Bridge writhes across the water

GOOD TO KNOW
HOLIDAY BASICS

ARRIVAL

GETTING THERE

You can drive to Amsterdam (or use it as a stop on a wider European road trip). However, the roads immediately around the city tend to get very clogged up so it is not the best way to arrive. There are park-and-ride options on the A10 ring road (including under Sloterdijk station, near Zeeburgereiland, at the Olympic Stadium car park, at Bos en Lommerplein and under the arena). Parking costs 8 euros per day for the first 24 hours and 1 euro per 24 hours thereafter. At the weekend and after 10am, the fee is 1 euro for the first day too. On top of this, you need to buy tickets to get into the city. For more information, check out *iamsterdam. com.*

Centraal Station is now linked to the UK via Eurostar and the Channel Tunnel *(eurostar.com)* and is also a great hub to explore cities in western and central Europe If you book in advance, there are excellent value Eurostar tickets out there.

Amsterdam Schiphol is one of Europe's biggest hub airports with plenty of flights to the UK and the USA. All major UK carriers fly to Amsterdam, and their fares can be very cheap. The airport is around 18km south-west of the city centre.

GETTING AROUND

From Schiphol Airport there is a train to Centraal Station every 15 minutes *(journey time around 20 mins, tickets 5.30 euros).* A taxi from the airport into town will cost about 45 euros. If you

The Magna Plaza shopping centre is centrally located in the old post office

are staying in a 4- or 5-star hotel, there is a KLM shuttle bus which runs every 30 minutes. Airport information: *tel. 0900 01 41 | schiphol.nl*

PUBLIC TRANSPORT

Public transport in Amsterdam consists of trams, buses and a few metro lines. Rokin Metro Station (line 52) is well worth a visit as they have created an exhibition between the escalators showing archaeological finds from its construction – including scissors, anchors and animal skeletons! Transport tickets are chip cards, which cost 3.20 euros for 1 hour and are valid for the whole of Amsterdam. It is better value to buy a day ticket or a multi-day ticket. Day tickets are valid for 24 hours, cost 8.50 euros and can be bought on board or using the machines at metro stations (and in

INSIDER TIP
Archaeology in the underground

some hotels). Multi-day prices: 48 hours for 13.50 euros; 72 hours for 19 euros; 96 hours for 24.50 euros. If you're paying on a bus or train, you must use a credit card. Note that on arrival at the airport, you can buy an *Amsterdam Travel Ticket* that also includes transport to and from Schiphol airport by train; it costs 17 euros for 1 day, 22.50 euros for 2 days or 28 euros for 3 days.

You should usually board the trams at the back door where the conductor sits. The rule for all chip cards is that you must check in when you board and check out again when you leave the tram, even if you are only changing lines. To do this, hold the ticket in front of the reader by the conductor's cabin or at the door, until the reader beeps. If you forget to check out, the ticket loses its validity!

Amsterdam Noord is served by buses and free ferries which all dock on the north side of the main station. Only the ferry to Buiksloterweg runs all night – the others run until about midnight. On weekdays, buses and trams run until around midnight, at weekends until about 1am. After that, there are night buses with special fares. A single ticket costs 4.50 euros and is valid for 1½ hours. *gvb.nl*

BICYCLE HIRE

Cycling in Amsterdam has its own rules so only attempt it if you are reasonably confident on two wheels. If you're up to it, it's the best way to get around the city. Costs for bike hire start at 10 euros for 24 hours.

🚩 *Star Bikes (De Ruyterkade 127 | tel. 020 6 20 32 15 | starbikesrental.com)*
Rent A Bike (Damstraat 20–22 | tel. 020 6 25 50 29 | bikes.nl)
Mac Bike (Weteringsschans 2, Leidseplein | De Ruijterkade 34b, main station | Oosterdokskade 149 |

Waterlooplein 199 | tel. 020 6 20 85 | macbike.nl)

All rental shops will have 👪 kids' bikes and adult bikes with kids' seats for little ones of all ages. But because most people ride without helmets in Amsterdam, getting one is not guaranteed so bring one with you if in doubt. You can also hire e-bikes – you won't see much benefit on Amsterdam's flat city roads but they are great for escaping the city.

TAXIS

Cab ranks can be found at places such as the main station, in front of big hotels and on major squares like Leidseplein. It's quite difficult to hail taxis on the street, as many simply don't stop. Even if the drivers tell you something different, you are free to choose which taxi you take! Electric taxis are also available. If you book with the *TCA App* (iPhone and Android), the price will be calculated before you get in. *Basic fare 2.95 euros plus 2.17 euros/km | tel. 020 7 77 77 77 | tcataxi.nl*

INSIDER TIP
Know how much it will cost

EMERGENCIES

CONSULATES & EMBASSIES
BRITISH CONSULATE
Koningslaan 44 | tel. 020 6 76 43 43 | ukinnl.fco.gov.uk

US CONSULATE

Museumplein 19 | tel. 020 5 75 53 30 |
amsterdam.usconsulate.gov

EMERGENCY SERVICES

Call 112 for the police, fire brigade
and ambulance.

HEALTH

If you need medical help, contact a
general practitioner *(huisarts)*. The
huisarts emergency service is available 24 hours a day: *tel. 088 0 03 06 00.*
There is also a special *Tourist Doctor* for
visitors *(Mon–Fri 8am–5pm, Sat
12–4pm | Singel 261 | tel.
085 2 10 01 01 | tourist-doctor.nl |
▥ F4)* and there is a doctors' practice
in the main station *(Central
Doctors | Mon–Wed, Fri 7.30am–9pm,
Thu until 10pm, Sat/Sun 10am–8pm |
De Ruyterkade 24 a | centraldoctors.
nl | ▥ G2)* which has its own phar-
macy. In the Netherlands, the
European Health Insurance Card
(EHIC) is accepted for EU visitors.
Everyone else needs travel insurance.

ESSENTIALS

CANAL TOURS ★

What would a trip to Amsterdam be
without a canal tour? There are a lot of
companies running these tours, most
of them starting from the main station
or in front of the Rijksmuseum. In
terms of route and prices, there is little
difference. Tickets can be purchased
online, but usually you won't have to
wait long if you just turn up, as the

Cyclists can do almost anything in
Amsterdam – including taking passengers

daytime tours start every 30 minutes.
They take you through the Canal Ring
and "Golden Arc", the Jordaan quarter,
out onto the IJ, into the Oosterdok
harbour basin and usually along a
stretch of the Amstel. Recorded
commentaries are given in English
and other languages. The price is
about 18 euros for 75 minutes
with, for example, *Rederij Lovers
(tel. 020 5 30 10 90 | lovers.nl)*;
*Amsterdam Canal Cruises (tel. 020 6
79 13 70 | amsterdamcanalcruises.nl)*;
and *Stromma (tel. 020 2 17 05 00 |
stromma.nl)*. They may not offer that
many tours but
Reederij Kooij have
the nicest boats and
their prices are fair.

INSIDER TIP
**Classy canal
tour**

*(Online ticket from 11 euros | Rokin
opposite house no. 125 | tel.
020 6 23 38 10 | rederijkooij.nl |*

F4) Evening cruises with or without a meal are also offered (see p. 80).

If you want to bring out your inner captain, you can hire a green electric boat from *Boaty* (*F7*). *(From 79 euros for 3 hours, max. 6 people | Jozef Israëlskade | walk 50m from Ferdinand Bolstraat along the Amstel canal | tel. 06 27 14 94 93 | boaty.nl | tram 12 Scheldestraat)*

There are also some specialist canal tour operators like those offered by *Rederij Lampedusa (every second Sat at 11am und 1.30pm | 25 euros | Dijksgracht 6 | rederijlampedusa. nl | tram 26 Muziekgebouw aan 't IJ) | Centrum).* They use boats formerly used to ferry refugees across the Mediterranean and tell the story of Amsterdam's history of immigration. *Plastic Whale (June–Oct, Sat 11am–1pm | 25 euros | various start points | plasticwhale.com)* ask you to get your hands dirty by fishing plastic out of the canal with them.

CUSTOMS

Unlimited goods for personal use can be imported and exported without paying duties within the European Union. If you come from outside the EU, strict restrictions apply, such as 250 cigarettes, 5 litres of wine and 1 litre of spirits (22% or more).

EVENTS

You can find a list of cultural events on the website *iamsterdam.com*. It is best to buy tickets directly from the event website. Same day deals same-day last minute tickets with a 50 per cent discount are sold at *lastminuteticketshop. nl*. The English-language *A-Mag* lists all kinds of events and is published every other month. It can be purchased from I Amsterdam Visitor Centres and many news agents for 3.50 euros, but many hotels and restaurants offer free copies.

INSIDER TIP
Last-minute tickets

GUIDED TOURS

Amsterdam is a good place to explore on foot. English-language tours through the historic districts are operated by big travel agencies and by companies such as *Local Experts (tel. 020 4 08 51 00 | local-experts. com)* and *TopTours (tel. 020 6 20 93 38 | toptours.net)*. Both companies also offer themed walking tours, such as through the red-light district and the *hofjes* in Jordaan. The price per person ranges between 15 and 25 euros, depending on the tour. *Arcam (tel. 020 6 20 48 78 | arcam.nl)* offers a great tour of the city's architecture every Friday afternoon from Easter to October.

Almost every bike-hire company offers guided bike tours. The most comprehensive tour programme, including trips out to the IJsselmeer, can be found from *Orange Bike (Buiksloterweg 5c | tel. 06 46 84 20 83 | orangebike.nl | ▢ G3)* and *Yellow Bike (Nieuwezijds Kolk 29 | tel. 020 6 20 69 40 | yellowbike.nl | tram 2, 11, 12, 13, 17 Nieuwezijds Kolk | ▢ G3)*. Prices are around 20 euros for 3 hours including bike hire.

There are also bus tours of the city from companies such as *Hop-on-Hop-off-Bus (daily 9.15am–6.15pm | 25 euros for 24 hrs | Damrak 26 | citysightseeingamsterdam.nl | 2 mins walk from the main station | ▢ G3)*, which stops at twelve major sights. Bear in mind that the streets of the old quarter are narrow, which means that buses can only go along the main roads.

I AMSTERDAM CITY CARD

The *I Amsterdam City Card* for leisure and cultural activities is valid for 24, 48, 72 or 96 hours. This chip card gives you a canal trip at a reduced price or even free of charge, use of public transport and free admission to several museums, such as the Van Gogh Museum, Amsterdam Museum and Stedelijk Museum. It also includes discounts for some other attractions and restaurants. At a cost of 60 euros (24 hrs), 80 euros (48 hrs), 95 euros (72 hrs) or 105 euros (96 hrs), it is only worth buying if you are going to get a lot of use out of it. It is sold online at *iamsterdam.com* and at *I Amsterdam Visitor Centres*.

I AMSTERDAM VISITOR CENTRES

I Amsterdam Visitor Centres provide tourist information and sell tickets for city tours. They can also help you find accommodation (for a fee). There can be long queues at their offices during the high season.

Stationsplein 10 (opposite the main station) | daily 9am–5pm, Sun 9am–4pm | ▢ G3

Schiphol Airport (arrivals hall) | daily 7am–10pm | tel. 020 7 02 60 00 | iamsterdam.nl | ▢ 0

You can also buy tickets for museums and events at the *I Amsterdam Store (Mon–Wed 8am–7pm, Thu–Sat 8am–8pm, Sun 8am–6pm)* in the northern waiting area at the main station. They also sell cool designer products and little souvenirs – like perfumes made from elm leaves, beer from local

INSIDER TIP
Station souvenirs

breweries, and scarves and hats made by local designers.

MONEY & PRICES

The currency in the Netherlands is the euro. Don't be surprised if you get only 50 cents change when it should be 52 cents because everything is rounded to 5 cents – 1- and 2-cent coins are rare. Payment by card is common, even for small amounts. In most restaurants, shops and supermarkets you can pay with a bank card and PIN code. However, some cafés and small restaurants don't accept credit cards. If you want to pay with a credit card, you must know your PIN. Prices for restaurants and hotels are expensive but not much different to the UK.

BUDGETING

Coffee	3 euros in a koffiehuis for a cup of koffie verkeerd
Beer	3 euros for a small draught beer
Cinema	11 euros for a ticket
Tulips	5 euros for 10 stems
Chips	2.50 euros for a medium portion with mayonnaise
Tram	7.80 euros for a 24-hour ticket

NATIONAL HOLIDAYS

1 Jan	Nieuwjaar (New Year's Day)
March/April	Good Friday, Easter Monday
27 April	Koningsdag
5 May	Bevrijdingsdag (only public institutions are closed)
May/June	Ascension Day, Whit Monday
25/26 Dec	Christmas

OPENING HOURS

On weekdays, most shops are open 9am–6pm, although some small shops do not open until noon or stay closed on Mondays. On Thursdays, city-centre shops stay open until 9pm. On Saturdays you can shop until 6pm, and on Sundays in the city centre from noon until 5pm. Supermarkets open Mon–Sat until 8pm and in the city centre Mon–Sat until 10pm, and Sundays until 8pm. Market stalls open until around 4pm.

PARKING

There is no free parking within the A10 motorway ring. Parking tickets are bought from machines. You can only pay by debit or credit card. In the city centre, it costs 7.50 euros/hr or 45 euros for a day ticket (9am–midnight). The fine for not getting a ticket is 55.50 euros. The much-feared wheel clamps are only used for repeat offenders. The fee if you do get towed away is 373 euros. *Car parks in Amsterdam city centre (approx. 40 euros/day): Europarking (Marnixstraat 250); Bijenkorf department store, Muziektheater (Waterlooplein), Nieuwezijds Kolk and Byzantium (Tesselschadestraat 1). Further information: parkerenindestad.nl*

PHONE & MOBILE PHONE

For the green telephone kiosks, which are becoming thin on the ground, you need a phone card – obtainable from a newsagent, post office or the tourist office (VVV). Codes: UK *0044*, USA *001*, Australia *0061*, Ireland *0353* Netherlands *0031*, Amsterdam *(0)20*

POST

Most post offices open Mon–Fri 9am–5pm, Sat 9am–1pm. However, there are fewer of them than there used to be. Stamps are sold in the *Bruna* chain of newsagents and at the checkouts in the *Albert Heijn* supermarkets. It costs 1.40 euros to send a postcard or a standard-sized letter to any place abroad. *postnl.nl*

TIPPING

In taxis, restaurants and cafés you round up the amount to be paid to make a tip of 5–10 per cent, and room service in a hotel is 1–2 euros per day.

WEATHER & WHEN TO GO

Amsterdam's weather is not exactly fabulous. It rains a lot and there can be a stiff breeze. But its coastal location means there are few days where it rains all day long. It is best to visit from spring to autumn but don't forget a brolly no matter when you're going!

WEATHER IN AMSTERDAM

High season
Low season

	JAN	FEB	MARCH	APRIL	MAY	JUNE	JULY	AUG	SEPT	OCT	NOV	DEC
Daytime temperatures	5°	5°	9°	13°	17°	20°	22°	22°	19°	14°	9°	6°
Night-time temperatures	1°	1°	3°	6°	9°	12°	15°	15°	12°	8°	5°	2°
Hours of sunshine per day	2	2	4	6	7	7	6	6	5	3	2	1
Rainfall days per month	14	11	9	9	9	9	11	11	12	12	14	13

Hours of sunshine per day   Rainfall days per month

DUTCH WORDS & PHRASES

SMALLTALK

Yes/no/maybe	ja/nee/misschien
Please/thank you	(formal) alstublieft, (informal) alsjeblieft/ bedankt
Good morning/afternoon/evening/night	Goeden morgen!/dag!/ avond!/nacht!
Hello/goodbye	Hallo!/Dag!
Bye	Doei!
My name is …	Ik heet …
What's your name? (informal/formal)	Hoe heet je?/ Hoe heet u?
I am from …	Ik kom uit …
Sorry	Sorry.
Pardon?	Pardon?
I would like …/Do you have …?	Ik wil graag …/ Heeft u …?

SYMBOLS

EATING & DRINKING

The menu, please	**De kaart, alstublieft.**
Could I please have … ?	**Mag ik …?**
Bottle/carafe/glass	**fles/karaf/glas**
Knife/fork/spoon	**mes/fork/lepel**
Salt/pepper/sugar	**zout/peper/suiker**
Vinegar/oil	**azijn/olie**
With/without ice/gas	**met/zonder ijs/ bubbels**
(Not) drinking water	**(geen) drinkwater**
The bill, please	**Mag ik afrekenen.**
By the window	**bij het raam**
The bill	**rekening/bonnetje**
Cash/debit/credit card	**kontant/pinpas/creditcard**

MISCELLANEOUS

Where is …? Where are …?	**Waar is …?/ Waar zijn …?**
What time is it?	**Hoe laat is het?**
Today/tomorrow/yesterday	**vandaag/morgen/gisteren**
How much does … cost?	**Hoeveel kost …?**
Where can I find somewhere with internet?	**Waar krijg ik toegang tot internet?**
Wifi	**wifi**
Help!/Caution!/Watch out!	**Hulp!/Let op!/Voorzichtig!**
Fever/pain/diarrhoea/nausea	**koorts/pijn/diaree/misselijkheid**
Pharmacy/drugstore	**apotheek/drogisterij**
Timetable/ticket	**dienstregeling/kaartje**
0/1/2/3/4/5/6/7/8/9/ 10/100/1000	**nul/één/twee/drie/vier/vijf/zes/ zeven/acht/negen/tien/honderd/ duizend**

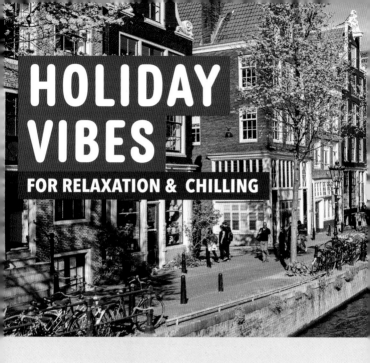

HOLIDAY VIBES

FOR RELAXATION & CHILLING

FOR BOOKWORMS & FILM BUFFS

PUBLIC WORKS

Based on Thomas Rozenboom's classic novel, which in turn was a fictionalisation of real events, this film tells the story of what happened when the authorities tried to build a new hotel opposite the newly completed main station. A stubborn violin maker refuses to let his house be torn down in place of the Hotel Victoria. Spoiler alert: the house is still there today! (2015)

THE EVENINGS

A recently translated post-war Dutch classic, *The Evenings* recounts mundane events from the life of Frits, an office worker. It is by turns funny and tragic and is a wonderful depiction of life in Amsterdam immediately after the war. (1946)

WAITER

If you want to get your head around Dutch humour, you need to watch at least one of star director Alex van Warmerdam's films. This black comedy tells the story of Edgar, a hapless waiter in a grim Amsterdam restaurant, who goes to the film's screenwriter to plead for a change to the plot. (2006)

PLAYLIST

0:58

‖ THE MAUSKOVIC DANCE BAND – THINGS TO DO
"Afro-Caribbean space-disco" is how the band describes its gloriously energetic music

▶ **SIMEON TEN HOLT** – CANTO OSTINATO
A minimalist piece of music composed in 1976, often played (as a duet) in the Concertgebouw

▶ **ANDRÉ HAZES** – MIJN LEIDSEPLEIN
A tragic love song to the Leidseplein from one of Amsterdam's most famous crooners

▶ **AMSTERDAM KLEZMER BAND** – A CHASSID IN AMSTERDAM
A Klezmer parody with many lyrics written in Dutch Yiddish

▶ **DE JEUGD VAN TEGENWOORDIG** – WATSKEBURT?!
Amsterdam hip hop at its weirdest

Find the playlist on **Spotify** by searching for **MARCO POLO** Netherlands

Or scan the code with the Spotify app

ONLINE

I AMSTERDAM BLOG
A blog run by the people who sell the I Amsterdam Card, it features current information on things to do in the city. *iamsterdam.com/en/blog*

AMSTERDAM FOODIE
An entertaining guide to eating and drinking in the Dutch capital with top tips for restaurants (sorted by type of cuisine) and general culinary observations. *amsterdamfoodie.nl*

RIJKSMUSEUM APP
The Rijksmuseum prefers this app to an audioguide. It works on most phones and is interactive, helping to make a museum visit more exciting for kids too.

FLATTIRE
Puncture and no bike shops in sight? This iPhone app allows you to summon help – for a fee they will come immediately. *flattire.nl*

TRAVEL PURSUIT
THE MARCO POLO HOLIDAY QUIZ

Do you know what makes Amsterdam tick? Test your knowledge of the idiosyncrasies and eccentricities of the city and its people. The answers are at the bottom of the page, and can all be found on pages 20–25.

❶ Which South American country was Queen Máxima born in?
a) Uruguay
b) Bolivia
c) Argentina

❷ How do you pronounce the river IJ?
a) Like the "e" in "me"
b) Like the English word "eye"
c) Like "idge"

❸ Amsterdam has an unusual mayoral office – what is it?
a) Red Light Mayor
b) Chips Mayor
c) Cycling Mayor

❹ Which of the following is a famous Dutch design company?
a) Droog Design
b) Nat Design
c) Fett Design

❺ Who first came up with the idea of living on boats in Amsterdam?
a) Sailors
b) Students
c) Merchants

❻ Which common housing feature did you once have to pay tax on in Amsterdam?
a) Windows
b) Shutters
c) Gutters

Houseboats are popular today. But who were the first Amsterdammers to live on the water?

7 **What are Dutch cyclists allowed to do?**
a) Everything
b) Ignore traffic lights
c) Ride two abreast

8 **What is Amsterdam's nickname?**
a) Western Warsaw
b) Svalbard of the South
c) Venice of the North

9 **What percentage of Amsterdammers cycle every day?**
a) Around 100%
b) 53%
c) 27%

10 **What is the name for the little poles that line streets in the centre of the city?**
a) Amsterdammertjes
b) Hollandertjes
c) Kaaskopjes

11 **What do the Oranje locks separate?**
a) Willem Alexander and Máxima
b) IJ and IJsselmeer
c) Amstel and Heineken

12 **What adorns Amsterdam's city crest?**
a) Two joints
b) Three crosses
c) Four tulips

13 **What are the hoist beams at the top of many houses used for?**
a) To get beer crates up to top-floor parties
b) To hang flags on for King's Day
c) To get bulky furniture into houses

INDEX

WE WANT TO HEAR FROM YOU!

Did you have a great holiday? Is there something on your mind? Whatever it is, let us know! Whether you want to praise the guide, alert us to errors or give us a personal tip – MARCO POLO would be pleased to hear from you. Please contact us by email:

sales@heartwoodpublishing.co.uk

We do everything we can to provide the very latest information for your trip. Nevertheless, despite all of our authors' thorough research, errors can creep in. MARCO POLO does not accept any liability for this.

PICTURE CREDITS
Cover picture: Shutterstock.com: high fliers
Photos: A. Bokern (143); DuMont Bildarchiv: T. Linkel (9, 17, 80, 113, 140/141); Getty Images: L. Patrizi (100/101), G. Tsafos (4), S. Winter (58/59); Getty Images/Atlantide Phototravel (128/129); Getty Imag-es/Image Source (131); huber-images: A. Armellin (38, 106/107), M. Borchi (126/127), K. Dadfar (43), R. del Vecchio (79), F. Lukasseck (138/139), S. Raccanello (44), M. Rellini (6/7, 40), R. Schmid (2/3); Laif: M. Gonzalez (85, 86/87, 91, 118), M. Gumm (74/75), T. Linkel (14/15, 26/27, 32, 52, 67, 122); Laif/Arcaid: A. Secci (54/55); Laif/hemis.fr: L. Maisant (70); Laif/Hollandse Hoogte: Burgler (10), C. de Kruijf (50/51), Engbers (22), B. van Dam (34); Laif/ Le Figaro Magazine: S. Gladieu (64); Look/age photostock (20/21); Look/SagaPhoto: (117), Forget (97); mauritius images: W. Dieterich (72/73); mauritius images/age: A. Leiva (37); mauritius images/Alamy (69); mauritius images/imagebroker: Mateo (12/13); mauritius images/robertharding (11); mauritius images/Westend61: (outside front cover flap, inside front cover flap 1, 8, 48, 94), D. Santiago Garcia (56/57); picture-alliance/ANP: M. de Swart (102/103), K. Paul (93), K. van Weel (82/83, picture-alliance/dpa: K. van Weel (104/105); picture-alliance/EPA: R. De Waal (24); Shutterstock.com: Luciano Mortula - LGM (25), Dutchmen Photography (132); vario imag-es/ Westend61: J. Kirchherr (98/99); Visum: E. van der Marel (46/47, 63)

5th Edition - fully revised and updated 2023
Worldwide Distribution: Heartwood Publishing Ltd, Bath, United Kingdom
www.heartwoodpublishing.co.uk

© MAIRDUMONT GmbH & Co. KG, Ostfildern
Author: Anneke Bokern
Editor: Christina Sothmann
Picture editor: Anja Schlatterer
Cartography: © MAIRDUMONT, Ostfildern (pp. 36–37, 120, 123, 129, outer wallet, pull-out map); © MAIRDUMONT, Ostfildern, using map data from OpenStreetMap, licence CC-BY-SA 2.0 (pp. 28–29, 31, 41, 45, 49, 55, 60–61, 76–77, 88–89)
Cover, wallet & pull-out map design: bilekjaeger_ Kreativagentur with Zukunftswerkstatt, Stuttgart
Page design: Langenstein Communication GmbH, Ludwigsburg

Heartwood Publishing credits:
Translated from the German by John Owen, John Sykes, Jennifer Walcoff Neuheiser
Editors: Anna Baildon, Kate Michell, Sophie Blacksell Jones
Prepress: Summerlane Books, Bath
Printed in India

MARCO POLO AUTHOR
ANNEKE BOKERN
A freelance journalist who has lived in Amsterdam since 2000, Anneke Bokern loves being by the sea and has learned to put up with people drinking buttermilk at lunch as her penance for this. She writes about Dutch architecture and design. When she is not in the middle of a project, you are most likely to find her at the Noordermarkt or putting its ingredients to use in the kitchen. She speaks fluent Dutch.

DOS & DON'TS

HOW TO AVOID SLIP-UPS & BLUNDERS

DON'T SPEAK ENGLISH STRAIGHT AWAY

Do try and learn some of the lingo. The Dutch are great linguists, and most people you meet will readily communicate in English, many of them fluently, and they don't expect foreigners to master their own language. Nevertheless, it often pays dividends to at least learn a few basics like "thank you", "good morning" and "please".

DON'T TAKE PHOTOS OF PROSTITUTES

It is not OK to take photos of women working in the Red-light District (and you may be soundly rebuked for doing so).

DO LEAVE YOUR CAR AT HOME

Driving in central Amsterdam is no fun at all. The streets are narrow, cyclists race past on all sides, lorries clog the roads and parking spaces are virtually impossible to find. Do yourself a favour and use a Park-and-Ride on the edge of the city – or just leave your car at home.

DO GET OUT OF THE CENTRE

There is so much more to Amsterdam than just the Canal Ring. Take a ferry to Noord, go to a restaurant in Oost and browse the shops in De Pijp to see some of its other districts.

DON'T ONLY DRINK HEINEKEN

Heineken, Amstel and Grolsch are Dutch beer brands that are available all over the world, which is exactly why you should try something else when you're in Amsterdam itself. The city is home to a few microbreweries that produce much more interesting beers. Have you ever heard of the breweries called Oedipus, 't IJ, or 't Arendsnest? Exactly!